North Korea
Kidnapped My Daughter

Sakie Yokota

Translated by Emi Maruyama and Naomi Otani

VERTICAL.

Published by Vertical, Inc., New York.

Originally published in Japanese as *Megumi, okaasan ga kitto tasukete ageru* in 1999 by Soshisa Co., Ltd.

ISBN: 978-1-934287-44-6

Manufactured in the United States of America

First Edition

Vertical, Inc.
1185 Avenue of the Americas, 32nd Floor
New York, NY 10036
www.vertical-inc.com

On April 27, 2006, a joint House subcommittee held the first congressional hearing on North Korea's abduction of foreign citizens. Mrs. Sakie Yokota flew to Washington, D.C. to testify. The interpretation transcribed below was provided at the hearing.

Chairman Leach, Chairman Smith, honorable members of the committee, I would like to thank you for this valuable opportunity to speak to you today. I am Sakie Yokota, the mother of Megumi Yokota, who was thirteen years old when she was abducted to North Korea in November of 1977, twenty-nine long years ago.

For twenty long agonizing years after Megumi disappeared while on her way home from junior high school, we didn't know what happened to her. It was 1997 when we finally learned that she had been kidnapped by North Korean agents.

Naturally we were immediately overjoyed with the thought that Megumi is alive and the hope of being able to see her right away. Since then nine more years have passed and I feel so profoundly sad and humiliated when I think about why we still cannot rescue her.

After years of lies and denial, at his meeting with Japanese Prime Minister Koizumi in September 2002, Kim Jong-il suddenly reversed himself and acknowledged the abduction of just thirteen Japanese. However,

Megumi Yokota soon after her kidnapping

Kim Hye-gyong in Pyongyang, 2002

the number of Japanese citizens that North Korea has abducted goes way beyond thirteen. Our list of suspected victims includes more than 450 cases. In the case of most victims, North Korea to this day refuses to acknowledge the kidnapping.

Of the thirteen Japanese it has admitted kidnapping, North Korea claims that eight of the victims are dead. Among those are my daughter Megumi, Ms. Yaeko Taguchi, Ms. Rumiko Masumoto, and Mr. Shuichi Ichikawa, all four of whose family members are here with me today. To support its contention of their death, North Korea handed Japanese officials several things, including a container of ashes it said were my daughter Megumi's remains. All of these things were thoroughly examined by the Japanese government, and all were judged to be totally worthless and unreliable.

This is the picture of my daughter Megumi taken in North Korea soon after her kidnapping. It was given to the Japanese government by North Korean authorities with the ashes in November of 2004. Megumi was a young girl who loved music and was always cheerful. But she looks so lonesome in this photograph that when I saw it I couldn't resist caressing her picture and saying, "Oh Megumi, you were here, in this kind of a place, how frightened you must have been. Please forgive me for not rescuing you yet."

In 2002 we learned of the existence of Kim Hye-gyong, Megumi's daughter and our granddaughter. Then in April of this year, another DNA test revealed that our granddaughter's father is actually a South Korean abduction victim himself by the name of Kim Yong-nam. Mr. Yong-nam was a sixteen-year-old high school student when he was kidnapped by the North. Beyond this, the victims of North Korean abduction include not only Japanese and South Koreans, but also citizens of at least twelve other countries including China, Thailand, Lebanon, and France.

In the case of my daughter Megumi, we learned of her abduction from a North Korean agent who later took asylum. He testified that when Megumi was kidnapped, "She was held in a small dark chamber in the bottom of a special intelligence ship where she scraped the walls with her fingers while crying out desperately, 'Mother, help me! Mother, save me!'—and that is how she was carried across the dark sea."

Even now, my daughter Megumi and other abductees must be alive somewhere in North Korea. We the families are fatigued both physically and mentally, yet we cannot stop as long as our own children are seeking our help.

We cannot recover the lost years for our children, but we can rescue the victims that were abducted from many countries of the world and allow them to spend the rest of their life in the lands of freedom. We must also not forget the North Korean people who suffered from the atrocities committed by their own government.

I plead now for all countries of the world to join us in saying that "we will not forgive the abductions—all of the victims must be returned immediately or we will initiate economic sanctions." This is a sincere wish from the bottom of our hearts from all of the family members here.

Members of congress, members of the administration, and people of America, thank you for your strong hearts and thank you so much for your help.

Rep. Jim Leach: "Well, thank you very much, Mrs. Yokota, and I am sure I speak for the panel when I say that you are a model mother and all of us wish you well. This is a problem of the world family, the American family as well as the Japanese family."

CONTENTS

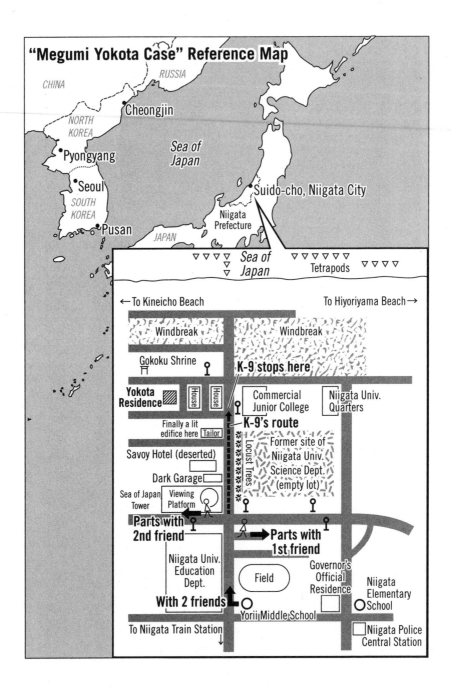

"Megumi Yokota Case" Reference Map

Chapter I
ONE DAY MY DAUGHTER SUDDENLY DISAPPEARS

The White Raincoat

Megumi disappeared during her second term as a first-year student at Yorii Middle School in the city of Niigata.

My husband worked for the Bank of Japan, and during his career our family was transferred many times. Before our marriage, he was posted in Sapporo. After our marriage, we lived in Nagoya, Tokyo, Hiroshima, Niigata, Tokyo, Maebashi, and finally, Tokyo again, at which point he retired.

He was transferred from the branch in Hiroshima to Niigata on July 23, 1976, about a year before Megumi's disappearance. Our family of five consisted of my husband and myself, our daughter Megumi, and Megumi's twin brothers who were four years younger. Upon our transfer to Niigata, we moved to a single-story residence that was provided by the bank. The house was located in the Suido-cho district.

We were far from the city center, but near the coast; the Sea of Japan was only a few minutes' walk away. Nearby was a vacant lot where the University of Niigata's Science Department building stood before it was relocated. A windbreak of trees lined the street, and at night the area became pitch dark. Having moved from the sunny city of Hiroshima, which faces the Inland Sea, my first impression of Niigata was that it was forlorn. When I mentioned this, my new friends in Niigata teased me, "You mustn't say that now during the height of the summer season when everything is bright and cheery. You'll see how forlorn the place can be when the snow falls."

"How long will father be posted in Niigata?" Megumi asked one day. I replied, "We have lived in each city for four to five years, so I think we will be here for about the same length of time." Megumi's response was a simple, "Ohhhh." Once or twice she said, "I wish we could go back to Hiroshima."

"This is a lonely sort of place, isn't it?" I would reply. As a parent, I probably shouldn't have said such a thing. But having left many good friends behind in Hiroshima, I empathized with Megumi's loneliness in the early days after our move to Niigata. For Megumi, the budding self-consciousness of adolescence must have made things harder—she seemed to become more reserved and shy among strangers.

The area where we lived was a neighborhood of

beautiful old residences. There were many grand homes nearby. Our house and the house to the left of ours had been built in the 1940s. A huge, single-story expanse, it felt like a vacation home by the sea. During the winter, we could hear the roar of the crashing surf, and at night, the window shutters would make a tremendous banging sound.

The bank also had an apartment building near our home for its officials' families. A friend who had moved into an apartment there once suggested that we move there also. However, this was the first time we had lived in a single-family residence, so my children liked the large yard where we could barbecue and they could run around and play badminton. Watching them play, I felt that this was more important, so we never moved.

The soil was sandy, but the garden was truly spacious. I enjoyed gardening, so it gave me great pleasure to go out and buy seedlings and flower bulbs; I planted many trees as well as tulips and narcissus.

Megumi transferred to the city of Niigata's public elementary school in the second semester of her sixth grade. She was by nature a very outgoing girl, so she soon became acquainted with the children of other officials at the bank as well as the staff of the Niigata bureau of NHK, Japan's public broadcaster. And gradually, her circle of friends widened.

In April 1977, Megumi entered Yorii Middle School and joined the badminton club at school.

Megumi had studied classical ballet since

kindergarten, and she enjoyed singing and drawing, so I had thought that she would join a club where she could pursue one of these interests. However, her close friends joined the badminton club and they decided that they would all play badminton together. So she joined the club in a very light-hearted way, but soon discovered that practice was very strict. She nonetheless threw herself into her new activity.

On the day my daughter disappeared, the weather was unusually warm and very sunny.

Every morning, a friend who was Megumi's doubles partner in badminton would come by our house and the two girls would walk to school together. On that day, as on all the other days, Megumi's friend stopped by our house. Though the day was warm, I thought that Megumi should take her raincoat with her—it would become chilly by the time practice ended and it was time to go home. I followed Megumi down the hall to give her the raincoat. The color of the raincoat was off-white.

Megumi paused briefly, then said, "I don't think I'll need the raincoat today. I think I'll leave it at home." I can't recall that her friend was wearing her raincoat, either.

Megumi called out, "Bye!" and headed out the front gate. That was the last time I saw my daughter.

"She Hasn't Returned."

No matter how late the badminton club practiced, Megumi usually came home around six o'clock. That evening, the clock read past seven but my daughter still hadn't come home.

There had been a badminton tournament for first-year middle school students on November 13, two days before her disappearance, and Megumi had been one of the entrants. There was a kind of post-tournament meeting on the 14th, so Megumi had left for school that day telling me, "I'll be a little late coming home today."

Although Megumi had told me in advance that she would be late, I had become worried when she didn't come home at six-thirty. I'd called the home of one of her friends who was also in the club to ask if the friend had come home. The road that Megumi walks from school is barely lit by street lamps, so I always worried at night until my daughter was safely home.

The friend's mother had reminded me, "The club had a post-game meeting today. My daughter just came home, so I am sure that yours will be home soon, too." I was relieved by her words, and soon enough, Megumi came home.

But Megumi did not say that she would be late when she left for school on the 15th, and yet she was late coming home.

Almost as if I were talking to myself, I said to my sons, "Megumi didn't mention that she would be late today. Did she say anything to you before she left?"

"She never said anything."

"It's getting late. I wonder what happened."

My anxiety grew.

"I'm going to school to see what's going on."

Leaving my two sons at home, I paused only to slip my feet into a pair of sandals and I was out of the door. As I was latching the front gate, I saw the elderly lady who lived next door.

"Where are you going at this hour?" she asked.

"Megumi hasn't come home yet, so I'm going to school to get her."

I began walking to school. I thought I would surely meet up with her coming home. Along the way I saw a man and a woman, and then perhaps two other people. But no Megumi.

I entered the school grounds, and as I looked toward the gymnasium, I saw a bright light inside and heard female voices.

Oh, the girls are still practicing, I thought.

I felt relieved and was about to go home again, but then I changed my mind. Wanting to make sure, I looked into the gymnasium through the doorway. The voices belonged not to students, but to grown women who were practicing volleyball. Cold fear ran down my spine and I felt more anxious than ever.

I ran to the main entrance of the school and found the night watchman standing nearby.

"Have the students who were practicing bad-minton in the gymnasium gone home?" I asked.

"They left a long time ago. All the students left a little after six," he replied.

An indescribable feeling of apprehension swept over me. Perhaps she had walked home along a different route. Perhaps she had stopped by a friend's house. I hoped against hope and ran as hard as I could back home. I peered through the bottom part of our front door, which is fitted with a clear piece of glass. Even before I opened the door, I knew Megumi's shoes were not there in the entryway, where they would have been if she were home.

To make sure, I called out to my sons who were watching television. "Has your sister come home?"

They came running to the front door. "No, not yet. What happened?"

"This isn't good. She isn't at school, either. This is giving me the shivers. I think I'll call one of her friends."

I immediately phoned the homes of some of her friends in the badminton club.

"I can't believe she's not home yet. We parted in front of the school, so she should be home by now. This isn't like her."

Every one of the friends I called said pretty much the same thing. I had a very bad feeling in the pit of my stomach. I called the badminton coach.

"I can't believe she isn't home yet," the coach said. "I saw her laughing with her friends in front of the school and she seemed to be her usual self. Maybe she stopped by the bookstore or something. Let's not make a big commotion yet; just wait a little longer for her."

Children in middle school sometimes like to stop somewhere on their way home from school. Imagine the embarrassment a teen would feel if he or she came home a little late to find the house in an uproar. I am sure that her teacher had such a scenario in mind when he counseled that we should wait a little longer.

At first, I believed he might be right. I told myself that she might have stopped by her orthopedic doctor's office where she was being treated for her knees. Megumi had been having growing pains and told me that it hurt when she did flexed-knee jumps during practice. She had been going for a while to a clinic on Furumachi-dori on the other side of town. I immediately called the clinic on the chance that she may have dropped in. But they checked their records and told me that she had not come in that day.

It was not like my daughter to stop by a friend's house or go shopping on her way home from school. It did not feel right, so I called her teacher again.

"She isn't home yet. This is the first time something like this has ever happened. Something about it doesn't feel right, so I am going out to look for her."

Her teacher immediately replied, "Then I'll go out and look for her as well," and quickly hung up.

I took my two sons and a flashlight and set out again in the direction of her school. Along the way, there was a hotel that had been damaged by a fire and was no longer in business, as well as an unlit parking garage. These were the places that I had always warned my daughter to be careful of. The Savoy Hotel outwardly looked like a normal hotel, but it was totally deserted and was therefore a place to be wary of.

I circled the area calling out, "Megumi, Megumi!"

When I still saw no signs of my daughter, I thought that she might be somewhere near the sea, so, pulling my sons alongside me, I retraced my steps and headed toward the shore. Across the next street was the Gokoku Shrine. Beyond the shrine grounds, across the street and through the stand of pine trees, was the sea. The grounds of Gokoku Shrine are not lit, and only the path that leads to the shrine itself glowed white in the inky darkness.

I was frightened, but there were three of us, and I had my flashlight with me, so I proceeded to enter the shrine grounds, calling my daughter's name as loudly as I could. I heard nothing. Even I was afraid to walk to the far side of the grounds and my sons began to cry that they didn't want to go any further, so we turned around and walked along the street that led to the sea.

There were several cars parked along the beach. I was desperate, so I flashed my light inside each car and asked, "Have you seen a young teen-aged girl?" I thought there was a chance that she might have been dragged into one of the cars.

The young people in some of the cars yelled at me. Of course, anyone would be startled to suddenly find him or herself in the glare of a flashlight. I immediately apologized, but my mind was in such a state that it didn't even occur to me to think that what

I was doing was very rude.

I also thought that she might have been locked into the trunk of a car, so I stood there for a while, watching. However, I had no idea how to open a trunk and my sons were saying to me, "You'll get into trouble if you touch those cars."

"But your sister may be locked up in one of the trunks," I replied. I felt a crushing sense of panic. I couldn't give up. Shining my light along the beach, I tried to see if I could find something that belonged to Megumi. I thought that she might have fallen from a sheer incline, but found nothing.

"I hope your father will come home early," I said as we went back to the house, not knowing what else we could do. When I got home, Megumi's teacher was standing by the front door, waiting for us. His home was nearby, so he had bicycled to our house.

"She's not home yet?"

"We were out looking but couldn't find her. I think we should call the police right away."

"Don't you think it would be better if we waited a little longer..." he started to reply as the phone rang. It was my husband. He wanted to let me know that he would be late coming home, as he was playing mah-jongg with his colleagues that night. The time was a little before eight o'clock.

The Police Dogs Stop in Their Tracks

That day, there was a welcome party at my husband's bank for a newly transferred official. Tea and cakes were served at the office, then a group of them decided to go out to play mah-jongg. My husband had phoned before taking his seat at the mah-jongg table to say that he would be late.

"Something is terribly wrong. Megumi hasn't come home yet. Please come home right away."

"That is strange. That doesn't sound good."

Promising to return at once, my husband hung up. He soon arrived by taxi with three of his colleagues. They all lived nearby, and were just as worried as my husband.

"She isn't home yet?" my husband said as he put his briefcase down. He and Megumi's teacher immediately set out to look for our daughter again. They searched all the places I had already covered but still could not find her. It was dark and the vacant lot was overgrown with weeds and shrubs, so even if there had been a shoe or something lying around, none of us could have seen it.

By the time my husband and Megumi's teacher came home, they had decided that it was best to call the police. I had thought that we called the police around nine o'clock, but the police log showed that the time of our call was approximately 9:50. In the meantime, Megumi's teacher went back to the school to look for her there once more on the chance that she had gone back to retrieve something and was locked inside the building, or perhaps had been unable to open the door in the lavatories.

On receiving our call, police from the Niigata Police Central Station as well as the East Station in the next district came right away to begin the search. They looked in the areas we had already searched: the vacant lot where the Science Department had been, the empty hotel, the grounds of Gokoku Shrine, and the stand of pine trees.

We were later to learn that Megumi was last seen around 6:35 p.m. After badminton practice, Megumi and two of her club friends had left the school around 6:25. The three of them had walked along the street leading to the sea.

One of Megumi's friends turned right at the second corner. Her other friend turned left at a large intersection with a traffic light. Straight down the street is the sea. To go to our house, you would turn left at the second street past the intersection, and then turn right at the second corner. Our house is the second from the corner, and it takes only a few minutes on foot from the intersection. There is a high stone wall on one corner of the intersection, so when Megumi and her friend parted, they were not able to see each other beyond it. It was around 6:35 when Megumi and her friend said goodbye to each other there.

Two police dogs also took part in the search. I put the pajamas that Megumi had worn that morning into a plastic bag and we took it to the intersection where

Megumi and her friend had parted. The two German shepherds began sniffing, then walked straight down the street toward the sea. When the dogs got as far as the corner where Megumi should have turned left, they stopped. They turned around and around but would not go further.

The dogs could not detect Megumi's scent beyond that point. The police could only confirm that she must have walked this far.

The search was called off at midnight, as flashlights allow one to see only a limited area. The police thought of every possible situation and called in a special unit that investigates kidnappings. The detectives put a tracer on our phone, and unmarked police cars were stationed near our house. That night, and for days after, my husband and I slept fully clothed near the telephone.

The search resumed at dawn, around 5 a.m. on the 16th. The mobile police unit from the Prefectural Police also took part in the search. The members of the unit stood a meter and a half apart and walked a straight line, using sticks to poke around the vegetation in the vacant lot of the university, on the beach and in the pine forest, but they were unable to find anything.

Every day, the police asked around each and every house in the neighborhood. And around the same time of day when Megumi disappeared, they stood near the intersection with her picture to question pedestrians. But no one had seen our daughter. Some of my husband's colleagues lived near us and would pass the area every day on their way from work. They told us that they were asked the same question many times.

A week passed without any attempts by anyone to contact us, so the police, concluding that this was not a kidnapping with ransom in mind, decided to make our daughter's case public. On November 22, the local newspaper published a large article on her disappearance, together with Megumi's photo. National papers also reported her disappearance in their Niigata regional sections. And the daily *Mainichi Shimbun* published a small article in an issue circulated nationwide. I think everything was done on the assumption that, whether Megumi was alive or not, she would be found within the city of Niigata.

We thought that media coverage would generate some kind of information, but we did not get any leads. There was nothing my husband and I could do, so we would go to the beach every day and see if Megumi's school bag or something that belonged to her might wash up on the shore.

All through that first week, before news of the search became public, my sons would cry and ask, "Where did Megumi go?" I felt a great deal of anxiety myself and was in a very emotional state. Only my husband was calm and composed. He gave us courage, saying, "She is all right. She will be back."

During the year following Megumi's disappearance, the police spent three thousand man-days investigating her case, but we were unable to gain any knowledge of what had happened to her.

Many detectives came to our home. One who came at the start of the investigation let it slip that there were "disturbing circumstances" surrounding the case.

He was referring to the 1965 kidnapping and murder of Kiyoko Orido, a young designer who had lived near the very intersection where Megumi said goodbye to her friend. It was a copycat crime modeled on the film *High and Low* by Akira Kurosawa, particularly the famous scene in which ransom money is thrown out of the window of a train in accordance with the kidnapper's directions.

In the Orido case, ransom money was demanded in a similar fashion. The young woman was called out of her house on the pretext that her car was parked illegally, and abducted. The ransom money was thrown out of the window of a train that ran between Niigata and Niitsu, but the victim was found murdered. Since the case had ended in tragedy, I think the detectives were worried that our case could end in a similar manner.

Because Megumi was still a child, everyone in the investigation truly worked hard.

The surf near the beach is lined with tetrapods to break the waves. If Megumi had fallen between these tetrapods, her body could not be seen from the beach. Patrol boats and helicopters were sent out to look along the beach from the ocean side. The following May, volunteer divers searched for her underwater.

The patrolman stationed near our house would stop by my home every day to inquire after us. While we lived in Niigata, the officer assigned to this beat changed three times, but Megumi's case was passed on from one to the next, and each officer made us his special charge.

At the time of Megumi's disappearance, the patrolman stationed near our house was a burly man who was an expert in *kyokushin* karate. Whenever we were transferred, he would telephone us to make sure we were all right. Later, when my husband was transferred to the main office in Tokyo and we were living in the Setagaya district, he was promoted to police sergeant. He came all the way to our house in Setagaya and said, "I have received two silver braids for my uniform and I would like for Megumi's mother to sew them on for me." The silver braids were hard, but I remember doing my very best to sew them on.

When Megumi disappeared, the chief of police of Niigata Police Central Station was a man named Takio Matsumoto. To this day, we exchange New Year's greetings every year. He once told us, "Megumi's case still remains very much on my mind. It pains me that we have not been able to solve it after all these years."

A key to solving this case was suddenly presented to us in early 1997 and became more widely known later that year when the weekly magazine *Shukan Bunshun* published an article entitled "Japanese Government Suppresses Concrete Evidence that Megumi Yokota Was Kidnapped by North Koreans" (May 1/8 1997

Double Issue). The article was based on an interview with a former top-ranking official of the National Police Agency.

In the article, the former official notes, "Successive top police officials possessed hard evidence of kidnappings by the North Koreans but suppressed it for decades... From the Prime Minister on down, the Japanese government also withheld these facts from the public. The police actually know which North Korean spy ship was used to kidnap Megumi Yokota."

I do not know the truth of the matter. And whatever took place behind the scenes, I do not think that the local police could have ever suspected that spies from North Korea had taken my daughter. My husband and I witnessed with our own eyes the effort that was put into the investigation, and we are grateful and confident that the local police did everything they could.

Was It an Accident? Did She Run Away? Did She Kill Herself?

My husband and I thought of every possible scenario that might explain Megumi's disappearance.

He thought that Megumi must have been involved in an accident at the spot where the police dogs stopped. There were no tire marks, broken glass, or traces of car paint on the pavement that suggested a car accident. However, Megumi could have been struck by someone driving without a license, or while intoxicated, or in the company of someone else with whom he or she did not wish to be seen by anyone, much less the police. In such a case, it was quite possible that the accident would not be reported, and Megumi might have been taken to a hospital quietly. In the worst case, if the driver thought that Megumi's injuries were fatal, my husband theorized that the driver had disposed of her body somewhere in the mountains.

The police also thought that the strongest possibility was either a traffic accident or abduction by a street gang. Dogs are said to possess a keen sense of smell, but I have heard that when the scent of a person becomes mixed with the scent of gasoline, the latter is so strong that the dog is unable to track down the human scent. It was very possible that Megumi had been placed in—or forced into—a car at the spot where the dogs stopped.

I also considered the possibility that she just wanted to be by herself, or had become acutely depressed about something.

As I mentioned above, there had been a badminton tournament for first-year middle schoolers in Niigata City on the 13th, just two days before her disappearance. Megumi had been chosen to compete and came in fifth in doubles with her partner. My husband and I were very happy with the result and told her that she had done very well. However, the level of girls' badminton in Niigata was among the highest in Japan, and Yorii Middle School ranked at the top. So Megumi was disappointed and said, "It's not good at all. At our school, fifth isn't even considered good." Perhaps she had been expected to take first place, or at least second.

The day before the tournament, the captain of the club had phoned to boost her confidence. I could feel how nervous Megumi was as she replied, "Yes, yes, I will do my very best." I realized that this was a very serious game for her.

Megumi had come in fifth, which was a disappointment for her, and others had placed first and second in the singles competition. Yet, Megumi was unexpectedly given a spot in the Niigata City special training camp.

She told me about it when she came home from her post-tournament meeting on the 14th. "I can't believe it. I've been chosen to go to the special training camp. Why would they choose me?"

During the tournament on the 13th, badminton instructors had come from Tokyo to watch the players. About ten of the first-year students, two from each middle school, were chosen to take part in the special training camp.

My daughter was not particularly athletic, but she was rather tall and strong since she was trained in classical ballet from kindergarten. Though she did not come close to winning in the tournament, perhaps the instructors thought that she had potential.

Taking part in the special training camp meant that she would be away from home. This would be the first time she would be spending nights away from home, training with people whom she had never met. I think that being selected made my daughter feel apprehensive.

"I don't think I'm fit for the camp. I wonder what I should do. Maybe I should tell them that I can't go."

"If you really don't think that you can do it, I think you should tell your club teacher right away. I'm sure there are others who would want to take your place, so you should tell him as soon as possible."

"Yes, but I'm afraid to say so to 'Snowman.'"

The teacher who had helped me look for Megumi was nicknamed "Snowman." He was a very good teacher, but it is still difficult to turn down a position for which you were chosen.

"If you are so worried, do you want me to come with you when you go and see your teacher?"

Megumi thought about this for a while but replied, "Well, I'm in middle school now. It will look funny if I have to have my mother come with me to talk to my teacher about something like this. If I'm going to tell him, I'll tell him myself. Anyway, I'll think about it a little more."

That was the end of our conversation regarding the training camp.

On the 15th, Megumi had set off for school her usual cheerful self. Yet when she was late coming home that night, the first thought that popped into my head was her concern over special training camp. Megumi is not the type of person to worry over something too much, but by then I knew that the club was very serious about badminton. Perhaps she felt so responsible about pulling her weight in the team that she had jumped into the ocean. The very thought sent me into a panic.

Of course, the juvenile division of the police department also considered the possibility of Megumi running away from home or committing suicide.

If Megumi had run away from home, the only destinations that we could think of were Hiroshima, where Megumi had good friends; the cities of Takasaki, Hitachi or Sapporo, where my husband's siblings lived; Kyoto, where I had grown up; or the island of Sado, which we had visited the previous year on a family vacation. We called friends and relatives, and the police checked the passenger list for the Sado Island Ferry, but there was nothing to suggest that she had headed to any of those places.

My husband had not heard about the special training camp from Megumi herself, so he was much more inclined to discount this possibility. All things considered, it was his view that there was little basis to think that Megumi had run away from home.

The circumstances supported his conclusion. For example, if she were to run away from home, Megumi would have thought to take her coat and her own clothes, but she did not do so despite the sure onset of cold weather. Her bank account deposit book and the watch that she wore during exams were also at home. It happened that, on that day, students were required to bring advance payment for their school trip, and Megumi had delivered this money in full. Also, the

15th was my husband's payday. The children always received their allowance on that day, so if Megumi had contemplated running away, she surely would have considered waiting a day—getting her allowance on the 15th would have increased her cash reserve. In addition, a book borrowed from the library had been due that day. Megumi had returned the book and borrowed another. It was just very difficult to believe that Megumi had run away from home right after badminton practice.

My daughter was mature for her age in that she read many books, including some relatively difficult ones. At the same time, she was still very much a child. Perhaps we were over-protective; for example, when she received cash for her New Year's present, she would hand the money over for her father to deposit into her account. On family vacations, she would carry her own ticket, but it was her father who made the plans, checked the train schedules, and purchased the tickets. Inexperienced as she was, she would not have been able to go far from home by herself. At the time, the Jyoetsu Super Express (the bullet train between Tokyo and Niigata) was not yet in operation, so there was little practical likelihood that she had left Niigata on her own.

Yet given the reality of her absence, I found myself hoping that she had run away. At least then there was hope that I would be able to see her again sometime, somewhere. I wanted to shut out of my mind the possibility that she had met with foul play at the hands of some awful person.

I once suggested to my husband that Megumi might have jumped into the ocean, but my husband thought that was unlikely, too.

Megumi could swim, but she had once almost drowned while taking swimming lessons. I think this happened when she was in fourth or fifth grade, when we were living in Hiroshima. Her school assignment over the summer was to learn to swim twenty-five meters. In Megumi's class, there were three children who could not swim that distance, and one of them was Megumi. I happened to have a friend who was well acquainted with a swimming instructor. When we inquired, the instructor readily offered to give Megumi private lessons.

It was when she had just started her lessons that she almost drowned, and Megumi became very afraid of the water. But her instructor was very good, and in the end, she was able to swim the twenty-five meters. On the first day of school after the summer holiday, Megumi informed her teacher that she had learned to swim. Her classmates teased her and said it couldn't be true, but she was able to swim the distance. Megumi proudly told me when she came home that she had surprised her whole class.

Though Megumi had learned to swim, I don't think it helped to alleviate her fear of water. My husband doubted that a child who was afraid of water would try to drown herself.

Since then, for twenty years, my husband and I

would talk about the things that could have happened to Megumi, and often feel despair that perhaps we had failed her as parents. We asked ourselves endless questions to which there were no answers. There was nothing that could assuage our sadness and pain, no target at which to vent our frustration.

Leaving Niigata with a Heavy Heart

After Megumi's disappearance, it became my husband's daily routine to walk along the shore. Every morning, he would leave the house a little early to search among the objects that had drifted to shore. His strength of purpose came from his conviction that even if Megumi were found dead and decomposed almost beyond recognition, he must be the one to find her.

I continued my own search as soon as I finished my housework each day. I would walk through a different part of town, going even to the industrial part of town. I walked everywhere, since I could not sit still at home. I would also take my two sons with me and walk along the shore calling Megumi's name. My young sons would complain that they were tired, but I would say, "Let's go a little further," and we'd walk for many miles.

It was especially unbearable at night. Every night, after my sons went to sleep, my husband and I talked about where Megumi might be, and I cried.

I changed the light bulb outside our house to a

brighter one and left it on all night. I was concerned that, should Megumi come home and find the light switched off and the front door locked, she would feel that her family had abandoned her. For six years, until our transfer to Tokyo, we lived this way.

The elderly lady who lived next to us was a very genteel woman and very kind. I think that she must be nearly ninety years old now. She was very concerned about Megumi and myself, and even now she sends us New Year's greeting cards. She knew that I loved flowers and frequently brought me armloads of magnificent purple hydrangeas, narcissus, etc. Whenever I see purple hydrangeas, I am reminded of this period and become very sad.

This neighbor once said to me, "Your light outside shines so brightly that I don't have to turn my light on in the house if I wake up to go to the toilet at night. But when I think of you doing this and waiting for your daughter to return, it makes me want to cry."

There was quite a lot of traffic on our street, since it was a shortcut to a larger one. Our street ended at the large thoroughfare, so cars would stop in front of our house once, then turn the corner to proceed up or down the larger street. Whenever I heard a car stopping in front of our house, I thought that Megumi had come home; I went to the window and peeked outside. I couldn't help it.

We could never know when we might receive a call, so we made sure that either my husband or I were at home at all times. My husband and I no longer went out together, and if there were family get-togethers, my husband attended alone. For twenty years, the four of us have never vacationed together as a family.

My husband's bank delayed his next transfer because of what had taken place. However, it was impossible to stay in Niigata forever because of what had happened. When our two sons were in the first semester of their last year of middle school, the bank proposed a transfer to Tokyo. It would be more difficult for our sons if we moved after they started high school. Equally strong, however, was the feeling that it would be emotionally difficult to move to another place where there were no reminders of Megumi, and I wondered what people might think if we moved away while the police were still investigating the case.

When I asked close friends for their advice, some said that it would be better if we started a new life in Tokyo. We had to consider our two sons, who were about to take the rigorous entrance exams for high school; for their sake, our friends advised us, the change would be good. Others said that if they were in our place, they would never consider moving to Tokyo. I didn't know what to do and the matter was constantly on my mind while I tried to decide.

The police assured us, however, that they would continue their investigation; we were not to worry, and could leave everything in their hands. I believe the police also reaffirmed that intent with my husband's employer.

I really felt as though I was leaving my heart behind me but, reassured by the words of the police, and also because I knew that I had my two sons to consider, I decided that we would move.

Near the day of our move, the neighbor next door asked if she could have the tiny camellia tree that I had planted. I was more than happy to give it to her, so our neighbor planted the little camellia near the entrance to her house.

Since then, in her yearly New Year's greeting card to me, my neighbor never fails to mention that camellia plant. This year, as always, she wrote to let me know of its bright red flowers. And each year, she writes, "Whenever I see that camellia, I cannot help but believe that Megumi is alive somewhere. I am sure that she is well."

In March 1997, soon after we were informed that Megumi was in North Korea, we visited Niigata and the kind neighbor who wrote these notes. The small camellia plant that had barely had a single bud had grown to reach the roof. The trunk had become very sturdy and I realized how much time had passed. That camellia had grown only little by little, but so many years had passed since it was a little seedling. The thought made me sad and I couldn't stop the tears from falling.

We heard that our home in Niigata was to be torn down after we moved out. Still, before leaving, my husband and I left a note with our new address. We wrapped it in plastic so that it wouldn't get wet, and tied it to the front door. We wanted Megumi to see it if she came back.

Then, we left for Tokyo. It was June 1983.

One day, only some ten days after we moved to Tokyo, a journalist from a women's magazine came to our house in the Setagaya district. She told me that she wanted to interview us about Megumi's disappearance. She thought there was a possibility that new information might come to light because the readers of the magazine were about the same age Megumi would be.

My sons were preparing for their high school exams at the time, however, and I did not want anything to distract them. I declined the interview and asked the journalist to please leave us alone for the time being. The journalist understood, but I realized then that though we may have left Niigata, interest in reporting about Megumi would continue.

There were no developments to shed light on Megumi's mysterious disappearance, and I had lived a life full of anxiety in Niigata. In some ways, moving to Tokyo made me feel that I had been freed because no one around me knew of her disappearance.

Niigata had been full of reminders of Megumi, and now the loneliness of separation increased with each day. The bustling streets near our new home were bright with neon lights, but there were days when I would pedal my bicycle down those streets sobbing all the way home.

Chapter II
HAPPINESS AT THE DINNER TABLE

A Vivacious, Happy Child

We had provided a photo of Megumi wearing her school uniform to the police and media. My husband decided to use that photo because it showed her in her uniform, with her school bag and wearing her school shoes, all the items she had on her or with her the day she disappeared. At the time of Megumi's disappearance, we never thought her whereabouts would remain unknown to us for such a long time. So it was logical for my husband to assume that if the police found her, if someone were to see her, or if she was otherwise found, she would be wearing the clothes that she wore the day she disappeared.

I know that my husband's decision was the right one, but the photo gave the impression that she was a shy, reserved girl. I said to him then and still think now, "Poor Megumi. Why are we using this photo?

Megumi in her middle-school uniform

With her school badminton club (standing, fourth from right)

"It makes her look melancholy. We have other, better photos that show the real Megumi, the happy Megumi. Those photos are better close-ups of her, too."

That particular photo was taken when Megumi was just recovering from rubella. The school ceremony marking her entrance to Yorii Middle School had taken place, but she had been unable to attend because her doctor feared that she could still infect others. My husband wanted to take a picture to commemorate the occasion and insisted on taking it while the cherry blossoms were still in bloom,* so a reluctant Megumi posed on the school grounds on a Sunday, before the first day of class. Megumi didn't want her picture taken because she still had pockmarks on her face, and she didn't like her hair since she couldn't take a bath while she was sick. Looking at the resulting picture, Megumi had pouted, "See, I told you. I look weird."

Because the photo was taken under these circumstances, I think the picture made Megumi look dispirited, giving the impression that she is a quiet, reserved girl. The real Megumi, however, was a vivacious, outgoing child who always said funny things and made people laugh. When she came home from school, she would chatter away and tell me all about what happened that day. Wherever Megumi was, there was laughter.

I remember that she had us laughing the morning of the day she disappeared. That day, my two sons were

* The school year in Japan begins in April.

going to get influenza shots at school, so I had to take their temperatures before they left. When Megumi saw me placing thermometers securely under my sons' armpits, she said, "If you keep the thermometer tight under your arm the way Mother is making you do, I'll bet the thermometer will stick to your armpit when you lift up your arm."

When the boys later lifted their arms, we saw that the thermometers were indeed stuck in place as she had predicted. The children whooped with laughter.

On another occasion, Megumi and I were riding the bus together. The man sitting in front of us had a nervous tic that was quite comical, and soon, Megumi was laughing silently to herself. When I saw what she was looking at, I started to laugh too, until finally, we both had to get off the bus because we could no longer contain ourselves. We laughed until our stomachs ached.

I admit it was a silly thing to do, especially for an adult, but being with my daughter made me feel light-hearted.

My happiest memories are of mealtimes at our house.

On my birthday and my husband's birthday, Megumi would buy us presents out of the small allowance we gave her. She would give it to us at the dinner table with a hearty "Happy Birthday!"

November 14, the day before her disappearance, happened to be my husband's birthday. Her present to him was a small comb, and she gave it to him with this message: "So that you can always look nice."

Another unforgettable present is a small brush she bought me for my calligraphy writing. We were still living in Hiroshima and there was a small stationer's shop that I frequented at the bottom of the hill where we lived. I often picture my daughter buying that small brush for me and walking up that hill in the heat, and my eyes always tear up.

My husband is not a loquacious person, and the boys are not by nature great talkers, so without Megumi at the dinner table it felt as though a light had gone out. It made such a difference that I have no words to describe the void I felt. It was unbearable.

Megumi was born on October 5, 1964, at Seirei Hospital in Nagoya. It was the year the Olympic Games were held in Tokyo, and I remember being able to sit up in my bed to watch the opening ceremonies. I was preoccupied with the birth of my baby, but I still remember feeling deeply moved that my first child was born in such a memorable year.

I wanted my children to have a carefree childhood, and felt it was important that they played outside as much as possible. When we lived in Hiroshima, a woman who lived in our apartment watched Megumi play in the sand and play games with other children in the garden of the apartment. She concluded with admiration, "Megumi is quite a genius at playing!"

She had seen Megumi devising lots of ways to play using nothing other than leaves, branches, and small stones. It was probably the ingenuity and imagination that children possess that impressed my neighbor.

Although my children played freely, I was strict about their manners. I impressed on them the importance of not hurting anything that was weaker or smaller than they, and to treasure every living thing, whether plant or animal. I consider myself fortunate that both Megumi and her brothers grew up into kind-hearted children.

When we lived in Hiroshima, there was a child nearby who was reluctant to go to school. I suggested to my children that they stop by and invite this child to go to school with them, since he lived along their route. The three of them did this, stopping every day for the child and reassuring him, "Everything is going to be all right," as they all walked to school together. Even now, the child's mother remembers this and tells me how much she appreciated what they did.

Our apartment in Hiroshima was surrounded by many hills. One day, an elderly woman was struggling up a hilly street with a lot of packages. Megumi told her, "I can help you carry some of your things home," and walked up quite a long hill with her. The woman was grateful for the help and gave her an apple, saying, "What a nice child you are." When Megumi came home and told me about it, she said that she felt badly about taking the apple that the lady had bought for herself.

In her first year in middle school, there was another student in her class who found it difficult to come into their classroom. Even on days when this student went as far as the school, she could not bring herself to go into the classroom, but went straight to the nurse's room. Megumi's teacher would tell my daughter, "Go and see how she is." So Megumi would go to the nurse's room and chat if the girl felt like talking, or reassure her and persuade her to come to the classroom. Megumi had a strong desire to do things for others, and when she had the opportunity, she always did her very best.

Torn from Her Home

Megumi disappeared, leaving just thirteen years of memories behind her. Some memories fade with the passing of time, but my memories of my daughter have become more concentrated, as it were, so that I recall every detail.

Megumi enjoyed drawing pictures, singing songs, and reading books.

She had what might be called a very bold drawing style. For instance, when she painted with watercolors, she never drew an outline. Rather, she painted freehand. I always thought it was interesting to watch her paint.

I think she was also a good singer. She never received voice training, but the music just seemed to flow from her because she loved to sing.

When my husband was transferred to Tokyo from Nagoya, we moved to an apartment in Omori. Megumi was still a toddler then, and I was busy unpacking, so an older woman who lived next to us kindly offered to look after her for a day. Later, she mentioned that Megumi had a great sense of rhythm. They were watching television together when Megumi took hold of the edge of the table and started nodding her head in time with the music.

After hearing that I started to pay closer attention. Indeed, when Megumi watched *Hyokkori Hyotan Island*, a popular children's program on NHK, she was stamping her feet and swaying with the music. I remember marveling at how she seemed to enjoy the music.

Megumi was singing all the time, in a clear, strong voice. I often sang along, harmonizing with her because she had a high-pitched voice and mine was lower.

Megumi also sang at her elementary school graduation in Niigata. After the school ceremony, the students held a thank-you party for their teachers. The entire sixth grade sang "Gypsy Life" by Schumann for the occasion. Megumi was in the chorus club and had been chosen to sing the soprano part, solo. She practiced at home and often said, "It's such a difficult part because the pitch is so high." Her teacher encouraged her in practice, saying, "I was right—you're the only one who can sing this part." Megumi's part really was rather difficult, and it went like this (the part in brackets was sung by another student).

Black-eyed maidens begin the dance
(Then, exhausted by the night's dancing, they lie

down and rest)
Those torn from a home where they were happy
See the beloved land in their dreams

Kuni Saito, the teacher who led the chorus club, recorded their performance. About a year after Megumi's disappearance, my older son brought home a tape and said, "Mother, the chorus club teacher said, 'This might bring back painful memories to your mother, but if she'd like to have it, here is a tape recording of Megumi's solo to remember her by.'"

I sometimes listen to the tape. The part where she sings "Those torn from a home where they were happy..." is especially wrenching and always brings me to tears.

After we moved to Tokyo, I joined the PTA's chorus club at my sons' new school. Whenever we sang the songs that Megumi had often sung, my heart would ache again.

Megumi also liked to read books. My mother often came to help me when Megumi was small, and it was she who noticed how Megumi showed great interest in picture books of animals, although she was barely old enough to stand. My mother advised that I start reading to her as soon as possible since Megumi showed such an interest in books. Megumi was overjoyed when I bought her two animal picture books, and though she wasn't able to talk well, cajoled me very expressively to read to her.

In this way I started reading to Megumi from when she was very small. In the beginning, it was fairy tales. I would read her the stories many, many times, and soon, she was able to repeat them word for word. I was surprised that, although she hadn't begun to read, she was able to recite all the words accurately, as though she had memorized the entire story by sight.

When I was expecting my sons, I read from *Japanese Folklore*. Some of the stories had illustrations here and there. They were typical folk tales, and there were many interesting ones.

At that time, Megumi had a favorite doll that had been given to her by her grandmother. It wore a small red cap and had arms and legs that dangled. She would carry the doll in one hand and the book of folk tales in the other, and would follow me, begging me to read to her. It was time-consuming to read her all the stories and I would often get tired, but Megumi never tired of hearing them.

When Megumi graduated sixth grade, she won a prize for borrowing the most books from the library, even though she had transferred to the school in Niigata in the second semester. She read all kinds of books, from comics, to works of literature not specifically intended for children, to detective stories.

Among the interests Megumi pursued over a long period was classical ballet, which she started to learn when she was a three-year-old in kindergarten. She kept it up until she entered middle school.

She became interested in ballet while we lived

in Omori. Her good friend was taking lessons, and her friend's mother had taken her to watch. I think she was quite dazzled by the dancing. After she came home, she said to me, "Me-chan wants to do ballet, too." "Me-chan" was Megumi's name for herself when she was small.

"Ballet is very difficult. Besides, you have two little brothers and I won't be able to take you to the lessons," I told her. But Megumi was undaunted and promised, "I'll practice really hard." I decided to go and observe a lesson myself. It seemed to me that the children were trained very rigorously.

Megumi was clever with her hands, but I didn't think that she would be able to raise her leg above her head or do splits. I continued to try to dissuade her, but in the end her persistence won out. I thought that she would soon tire of her lessons, but she continued dancing until she entered middle school.

When we moved to Hiroshima, Megumi continued ballet lessons at a studio where the prima ballerina Yoko Morishita first studied. It was recommended to me as a good ballet school. I asked Megumi if she wanted to continue in Hiroshima; she did, so I enrolled her.

Lessons were held once a week and the discipline was very strict. Since the studio trained many professional dancers as well, instilling professionalism was part of the instruction. The instructor taught with a cane in one hand that was used to tap out the beat on the floor. The instructor also corrected the students' manners and taught them to behave respectfully. It was wonderful training.

Every few years, the school held a recital. It invited professional male dancers and selected the most advanced students in class to perform the lead roles in major works such as *The Nutcracker* and *Sleeping Beauty.* Megumi took part in several recitals with the other students. Although their parts were small, they still had to work hard. Any dancer who was out of step with the others received a scolding.

Whenever I went to pick Megumi up, I would observe the lessons and saw that the instructor was very strict. I even wondered sometimes if I should not have steered her toward singing lessons instead.

Badminton, which Megumi started in middle school, demands an entirely different set of muscles than ballet. In ballet, the movements must be graceful and smooth, but badminton requires bursts of power to hit the shuttlecock. It was too strenuous to pursue both, so Megumi had to choose.

Her ballet teacher thought it would be a pity for Megumi to quit, but in the end Megumi decided on her own not to pursue ballet anymore since she had become a member of the badminton club. After her last recital, Megumi quit ballet in August, three months before her disappearance.

Megumi had a sense of responsibility towards others. She was also becoming more introspective, as we can see in the following essay she wrote about her future:

At this time, I haven't given any special thought to what I would like to do in the future. Maybe this is why I'm very motivated to study. It is a mystery, even to me, why I am not thinking more seriously about my future. But when I look back, there are reasons that may explain why.

When I was small and growing up, my head was full of fantasies, like becoming a nurse, or a beautiful bride. But every two years or so I changed my mind. First I wanted to be a bride, then I wanted to be a nurse, then a singer, and so on. I realized what was happening when I was in fifth grade. Since then, I've been convinced that I'll probably soon change my mind again. So even if I were to say, "I would like to be such and such in the future," I will probably change my mind in three years or five years, and I will find myself heading in a totally different direction. That is why I cannot say for certain, *this* is what I want to be in the future. But if I have to think seriously about what I would like to do, I think it is important to make a decision based not on outward appearances, as I did when I was small, but on whether it is suited to my abilities. My ideal is to shape a future for myself that connects my abilities, my dreams, and reality.

(From a composition written in sixth grade)

With the end of elementary school on the horizon, perhaps she had begun to think about herself more objectively. It was a sign that she was leaving her childhood fantasies behind her.

Megumi was forced by circumstance to head in a "totally different direction." I wonder what kind of woman she would have become if she had grown up without becoming entangled in this incomprehensible affair.

About Our Dog, Lily

In sixth grade, Megumi belonged to a school club that took care of the plants and animals at school. She loved both plants and animals, and although she wasn't fond of snakes, she showed no fear of frogs or worms even when she was small. Other children would shriek that they were creepy and run away, but Megumi used to calmly put a worm on her hand and say that it was "cute."

When we lived in Omori, Megumi often brought home abandoned cats because she felt sorry for them. We lived in a rented apartment, so we were not allowed to keep dogs or cats. But Megumi would make a bed out of a cardboard box and put it in a shed in the garden where she secretly took care of her cats. In the morning, Megumi would run out to give the current resident some milk, and in the evening she would surreptitiously let it out in the garden to play. She thought it was her secret, but I think everyone who lived in the apartment knew. If a cat meowed at night, I was sure to hear the next day, "Did Me-chan pick up another stray?"

Both Megumi and her brothers liked animals, and from the time they were all small they wanted to keep a dog or a cat. However, we always lived in rental housing provided by the bank, so the best we could do was to keep a bird. When we moved to the house in Niigata, the children thought that we would at last be able to have a dog, but it was difficult to consider having a pet since my husband's work entailed a lot of moving about.

Then, Megumi disappeared. My sons would not always say so in words, but they were worried about their sister and looked sad. My husband and I decided that if we adopted a dog, it might lift their spirits and give them something else to think about.

We needed to discuss what type of dog we wanted, so the boys bought a book. At the time, a breed known as the Shetland sheepdog had become very popular. Looking at the pictures, my sons decided that this was the handsomest dog and it was settled.

The boys and I went to a pet shop that was recommended by another family we knew through my husband. We chose a healthy female puppy and named her Lily. The puppy whimpered for its mother, so I wrapped an alarm clock in a towel and put it in the doghouse with her.

She was a pampered dog. Even after she was grown, she would sleep at night on a towel that we placed at the foot of our futon mattress. My husband, especially, doted on Lily and would take her out for a walk every day, searching along the shore and on the grounds of Gokoku Shrine for anything that might have belonged to Megumi.

Lily had a long and silky coat. Whenever we took her out, women and children would come up, pet her, and exclaim, "What a beautiful dog!" Lily understood, and would wag her tail with all her might. She was a friendly dog.

We once entered her in a contest, and she won second place in the category for all breeds under the age of six months. She came home with an impressive medal. We used to laugh and say that she was the only one in the family who had won a medal.

When we were transferred to Tokyo we feared that we would have to give her up because it was difficult to find a house that allowed us to keep pets. An acquaintance offered to take care of her, but luckily there was a single-family house available in Setagaya and we were able to take Lily with us. Lily was in the prime of her life while we lived in the house in Setagaya. Sometimes, when my husband took Lily out for a walk, they didn't return for two hours.

Since Megumi loved both dogs and cats, I regretted not having allowed the children to have a pet earlier. Our family used to say that it would be nice if Megumi came back while Lily was with us.

After Lily passed the age of ten, she began to weaken, troubled by injuries on the paws of her feet and suffering from ear infections. By the time we moved from Tokyo to our next posting in Maebashi, Lily had become progressively weaker and her coat had begun to lose its luster.

Soon after Lily turned fifteen, a lump was discovered on her back. We had it surgically removed since we were advised that, left untreated, it would prevent her from walking properly. However, the operation only spurred the tumor to spread. In the end, she had trouble urinating because of bladder problems, and blood showed up in her stool because of stomach problems. It's painful to recall this period because Lily suffered so much. Towards the end, the entire family nursed her around the clock, but her time had come. Lily died about three months after my husband's retirement.

Lily had lived with us for fifteen years and seven months. We lived with Megumi for thirteen years, so our time with Lily was longer than that with our daughter. The entire family had hoped that Megumi would come home and be able to meet Lily, but this wish was not granted us.

The Ties of Siblings

Megumi's twin brothers were born when we were living in Omori. Megumi was in kindergarten at the time. Since a lot of her friends had younger brothers and sisters, Megumi repeatedly said, "I wish I had a baby."

The school bus that took her to and from kindergarten stopped in front of Kashima Shrine. One day, when I went to the bus stop to pick her up, Megumi got off and suddenly announced, "Me-chan is going to ask for a baby," and dashed towards the shrine. She clapped her hands together in front of the shrine and said earnestly, "Please give Me-chan a baby."

You can imagine Megumi's delight when she became a big sister to not one, but two brothers at once. I was in the hospital for a while, but I later heard that Megumi had walked around the grounds of our apartment proclaiming loudly, "Me-chan has two babies now."

I was still in the hospital when, one day, Megumi popped into my room.

"Did you come with your father? Did he take the day off today?"

"No, I came with Mari."

"Who's Mari?"

A young woman came into my room and introduced herself, saying, "I'm sorry to surprise you. Nice to meet you." Mari was the sister of my next-door neighbor. She was visiting her sister and had become acquainted with Megumi.

"Megumi told me that she wanted to visit you. I was worried, so I came with her. I'm really surprised that she remembered the way, even though this hospital is quite a distance from your home."

Our apartment was along the Keihin-Tohoku line, near Omori station. From Omori, we would walk in the direction of the next station, Oimachi, but the hospital was much further on, near Oimachi itself. It would take a child about twenty minutes to walk from the apartment.

My daughter had visited me at the hospital before, but it had always been with my husband. Since my mother had told Megumi that she must not go by herself, she had probably asked Mari to come along. Mari had walked all that long way with Megumi, holding her hand.

I was very surprised to receive a visit from someone I had never met before. My neighbor, on the other hand, was worried because she couldn't imagine where Mari could have gone, but this I only heard later.

Megumi had walked that long distance because she wanted to see her mother, as well as the brothers she had longed for so much. I now frequently ride the train that runs along the road Megumi walked that day. I picture my daughter in her pigtails adorned with ribbons, walking hurriedly to the hospital holding on to Mari's hand, and my heart aches.

I believe that Megumi and her brothers were very close.

My older son took violin lessons when he was in elementary school, but started badminton when he entered middle school and continued to play in university. My younger son started swimming in middle school and continued to swim in university as well. I think it was due to Megumi's influence that both my sons pursued sports.

My older son was married in October 1997, the year

we learned that Megumi was alive in North Korea. At the wedding reception, we had a place set for Megumi at the table and arranged for a meal to be served at her place as well. As we sat looking at Megumi's empty seat, all manner of thoughts, both bitter and sweet, passed through our minds.

When we learned where Megumi was, our younger son was working in Nara. He related to me later that thinking of Megumi's plight made him so sad that his eyes filled with tears and he could hardly see well enough to drive.

My sons had always held back their own tears, no matter how much they wanted to cry. One time I felt so despondent that I cried as I cooked dinner. My sons came and stood on either side of me, both of them waving fans and saying, "Mother, you must feel hot in here."

I sometimes asked my sons, "What do you think has happened to your sister? I just don't understand what could have happened." Of course, my sons had no answer when they were children. However, by the time they were in university and had become old enough to make their own judgments, they would say, "She has been missing for a long time, yet nothing that belongs to her has ever turned up, and no one has ever seen her." They had reached the conclusion that Megumi had been "caught up in the middle of something really powerful."

After we discovered that she had been abducted, I learned that my older son had turned to the Internet to send messages. His message read, in part, "An abominable crime had taken place, and yet, for twenty years the Japanese government did nothing." He sent this message to Ryutaro Hashimoto, Prime Minister at the time, Keizo Obuchi, the present Prime Minister, and Masahiko Koumura, Minister of Foreign Affairs, as well as to President Clinton. His message was harshly worded, so I once cautioned him that he was too young to use that kind of tone.

I received a call from Ryozo Kato, then Asian Bureau Director of the Foreign Ministry, who said, "I've had the honor of receiving a message from your son." I knew that the message was very critical of the government, so it could hardly have been an "honor" to receive it. I said with great deference, "Please excuse my son for being so outspoken." But I found out then that the director had read my son's message.

Before then my sons had never spoken about what had happened. But I think their anger was all the more powerful because they had bottled it up for so long. I believe the brothers and sisters of others who were abducted to North Korea all feel the same way. Many of the siblings have chosen to take the place of their aging parents in making a powerful appeal to rescue their loved ones.

It may sound strange for me to say that I feel grateful for what we have endured. But I do believe that my sons have learned to be perceptive because they experienced hardships not known to children who have led happy lives growing up in a normal household. I want to believe that there are positive aspects to what has happened, at least in terms of the opportunity that this experience has given them to develop spiritual strength within themselves.

Grandfather, Please Don't Be Sad

Megumi's abduction wasn't a hardship only for our immediate family. It was equally difficult for my husband's father who lived in Hokkaido, and my brother and his wife who lived in Kyoto. My brother and his wife loved Megumi as though she were their own child, and she had always returned their affection.

I lost my own father when I was in middle school, and both my mother and my husband's mother passed away before Megumi's kidnapping. My mother had often looked after Megumi when she was little; if she were alive now and knew of all this, it would have saddened and distressed her deeply. The same can be said of my husband's mother, who passed away at about the same time as mine.

But my husband's father was not spared this sadness. He had studied Chinese classics in university and taught language arts in Hokkaido. He also wrote many books of *tanka* poems. After his retirement, he took great pleasure in visiting his children once a year at their homes on the main island of Japan. Along the way, he would stop by places associated with Japanese literature, such as Tono in Iwate Prefecture, the setting for Kunio Yanagida's *Legends of Tono*. In October 1977, just a month before Megumi's disappearance, he had visited our house in Niigata with a copy of *Snow Country Tales* by Bokushi Suzuki. When he left, we went to Niigata Airport to see him off; that was the last her grandfather saw of Megumi.

Two years before that visit, Megumi's grandmother in Hokkaido passed away. We went to Hokkaido for the funeral and stayed with my father-in-law at his house for four days. Since all the grandchildren were there, Megumi and her cousins were able to play together and enjoy their stay. But in the morning, Megumi went out by herself to help her grandfather shovel snow. It was her first experience doing so and she probably found it fun.

When we were ready to return home, we called a taxi and my father-in-law came to the doorway to see us off. Megumi called out, "Goodbye, grandfather" and started towards the car. As we were getting in, her grandfather called out, "Take care of yourselves." When she heard this, Megumi dashed back to her grandfather to give him a hug, and said with tears in her voice, "Grandfather, are you going to be alone? Please, don't be sad. Please take care." Hearing Megumi's words, tears began to roll down my father-in-law's face.

He worried over Megumi's fate until the last. He died on March 26, 1997, two months after he heard that she was being held in North Korea. He was ninety-three years old. He had been ill from the previous year and, when winter came, was admitted to a hospital in Tomakomai run by my husband's brother, who is a doctor. I think that hearing what had happened to Megumi was a huge blow to him. My husband and I suddenly had much to do after we learned of Megumi's true whereabouts, so we were not in time to say good-bye.

Hearing of his passing, we rushed to Hokkaido to be at his wake. According to my husband's brothers and sisters who were at their father's bedside, his words toward the end were, "We must take good care of the soldiers returning from the war." My in-laws could not fathom the meaning of his words at first. At the end of the last war, my husband was still in his first year of middle school, and neither my father-in-law, my husband's brothers, nor any of their close relatives had fought in the war. They concluded that the "soldiers returning from war" must have meant Megumi, who was far away across the sea.

My husband and I agree with their interpretation. When my father-in-law heard that his granddaughter, missing for 20 years, was in North Korea, it must have instantly brought to mind the dangers of war.

Megumi was the apple of her grandfather's eye, and when I think how cruel and painful it was for my father-in-law to hear of Megumi's fate, my heart goes out to him. I feel my father-in-law's boundless love for Megumi when I realize that his last thoughts were of his granddaughter's future, a future when she would safely be back in Japan.

Chapter III
SEARCHING FOR LEADS

Call from a Bogus Kidnapper

Ever since Megumi disappeared, not a day has gone by without my husband and I feeling impelled to look for our daughter. We wanted to do everything we could as parents, and we were driven to somehow find her ourselves. I constantly felt as though Megumi were reproaching us and asking, "Mother, Father, why aren't you looking for me?"

Until I learned that Megumi was in North Korea, I believed that Megumi had disappeared of her own free will. I had come to think that she was alive, living somewhere, because there simply wasn't a single clue that could convince me otherwise. And if she did leave on her own, I tried to think of all the things that might have motivated her to do so.

Before her disappearance, over the summer holidays, Megumi had seen two movies with her father, *Take*

All of Me and *The Cassandra Crossing. The Cassandra Crossing* was a film bursting with action and special effects, while *Take All of Me* was a sad but uplifting movie about a girl who dies of leukemia. A friend of Megumi's had recommended that she go to see it. My two sons wanted to watch an animated feature, so I had taken them to another theater.

I remembered that Megumi had come home in raptures, telling me as soon as she came in that *Take All of Me* was a wonderful movie. I thought that if Megumi had run away from home, perhaps there had been something in the story that had motivated her. I decided to go and see the film myself.

It was a love story about a pianist who has fallen on hard times and become a piano player at a disreputable bar. He falls in love with a young girl who is sick with leukemia and does not have long to live. He is inspired by her fight to survive and, through her, regains his own sense of worth. The film was both moving and beautiful, and the background music was memorable as well. I could see why it would strike a chord in an impressionable young girl. I also felt relieved as I left the theater, because there was nothing in the movie that could have motivated Megumi to leave home.

As I mentioned before, Megumi had loved to draw since she was a little girl. She was particularly good at drawing female characters similar to those in manga comics. When I searched Megumi's room, I found a pamphlet from an art school, and I immediately contacted them. But there was no one registered who fit Megumi's description. I thought there was also a chance that she may have found a manga illustrator who had taken her under her wing. When I went to bookstores, I would search among manga books for illustrations that were similar to Megumi's. This has become a habit since her disappearance.

About two months after Megumi's disappearance, in January 1978, we became the victims of a cruel prank.

On that day, I think it was a little before noon, the phone rang and the caller asked, "Is this the Yokota residence?" When I replied that it was, the caller said, "I have Megumi with me." I was so surprised that my legs began to shake.

This man has kidnapped Megumi, I thought. I was shocked by the call, but at the same time it gave me hope because I thought that at last I would know my daughter's whereabouts.

By then, the tracer on our telephone had been taken off and the police were no longer stationed nearby. However, my younger son was with me because he had stayed home from school with a cold. I told the man, "Please wait a moment," and I motioned for my son to come to me. I gave him a memo that read, "Phone call from kidnapper. Call police. Go next door."

My son had a fever and was probably cold. He was trying to put something on over his pajamas, so I signaled with my eyes for him to hurry. The kidnapper became suspicious and snapped, "Somebody's there with you," so I told him, "My little boy is sick. He stayed home today from school." When I emphasized that he was a small child, the man seemed convinced.

My neighbor slipped into my house with my son after contacting the police. A friend, whose daughter had been a good friend of Megumi's and who had come to see me often after Megumi's disappearance, also happened to visit me that day. The two of them sat quietly by my side, listening to every word I said. Since my husband was away at work, it's impossible to overstate how reassuring it was to have them near me.

The police soon arrived with their tracer and quietly attached it to my phone. The detective signaled me, "Try to prolong the conversation. Keep talking." The police had told me before that it took time to trace a call, and they had taught my husband and me techniques to prolong the conversation. For instance, I was to say that I didn't understand exactly where to take the ransom, and get the kidnapper to provide further details.

But the man on the phone didn't say a word about a ransom. I was desperate to continue the conversation.

"How old are you?" I asked.

"It doesn't matter how old I am!"

When the man shouted at me angrily, I could hear my voice cracking from fear and tension, but I did my best to stop shaking and tried to talk to him. I asked him where Megumi was, and also what she looked like. The man answered my questions and gave me clear answers: he had met her near Niigata station, and now had her working at a noodle shop.

When I looked toward the detective, he still made motions to "keep talking."

"You sound like a very young man. Why are you doing something that will make the police come after you, when you have so much ahead of you?"

I continued, "People are much happier when they have nothing to hide. If you like Megumi so much, I will let her marry you. We could all live together as a family."

Hearing my words, the man began to sound a little wistful; his tone became calmer and he continued to answer my questions. At last, he mentioned an amount, 5 million or 8 million yen—I don't remember the exact figure—and said nine o'clock that night. He instructed me to bring the ransom to nearby Hiyoriyama Beach, and to come alone. I promised him that I would somehow get the money and that I would be there.

I had been talking to him for an hour. I didn't realize it until later, when someone told me, because it didn't feel as though an hour had passed since the phone rang.

In the meantime, the police had been able to trace the call to the man's own apartment. Since the door was unlocked, the police were able to go in and apprehend him just as he was about to put down his phone. According to the police, newspapers with articles of Megumi's disappearance were strewn all around the telephone and the man had been looking at them as he talked.

When I received word of his arrest and the detective praised me for keeping the suspect talking for so long, I felt so weak I could barely stand. At the same time, I felt relieved because now all we needed to do was ask the kidnapper where Megumi was.

But the kidnapper turned out to be a high school student playing a cruel joke. From his voice I had imagined him to be twenty-six or seven years old, so his youth was the first surprise. Then I was told that he had only pretended to be the kidnapper. He confessed that he had read of her disappearance and decided to make the bogus call.

I wasn't immediately convinced that it was a hoax. He had actually given me the name of a noodle shop, and had said that he was making Megumi work there. We quickly verified that there really was a noodle shop by that name, so the detective who had come to my house immediately contacted the Central Police Station to follow up. However, the police discovered that the caller's claims were false. Despite their conclusion, it was difficult for me to be so easily dissuaded. I thought that there might be a connection between the student and Megumi's disappearance, and begged the police to investigate thoroughly.

The police held the student in custody for a week or ten days and questioned him thoroughly, but we received word that he was not connected to the disappearance. Because the call had given me hope, the news from the police was devastating. I wept.

The phony kidnapper was a high school student

and an only child. Since both parents worked, perhaps he was just lonely. The detective later told me that the student tearfully admitted to police, "No one has ever told me that they wanted me to live with them." Yet, at the same time, I never received a letter or visit from either the student or his parents apologizing for what he had done. It was an incident that felt like a twisting of the knife already plunged into our hearts.

She Looks Like Megumi!

We did everything we could do to look for Megumi. We all but flew to any source of information that we thought might lead to her discovery.

The daytime tabloid programs had a segment titled "Have You Seen This Person?" People would appear on the program and tell their story to the viewers, hoping for information on missing family or friends. While we lived in Niigata, we went on this type of show four times, each time with a photo of Megumi. A reporter for the show would come to our house to shoot this segment. We were on "The Hiroshi Ogawa Show," "The Mizoguchi Morning Show" (twice), and "Look, Look—Konnichiwa." They are quite widely watched; even the phony kidnapper had claimed that he had watched one of these shows with Megumi although, of course, we later learned that it was a lie.

Unfortunately, our appearance on these shows did not yield any new information.

While we lived in Niigata, we also went to the police station once a year to look over photos of unidentified bodies. Every year in mid-August, the police made the photographs available to the public for a week. It coincided with the Bon Festival (the Buddhist festival for the dead) and I think it was an effort to step up identification of these victims. In Megumi's case, the police already had her fingerprints and other detailed information, so there was little chance that anything would escape their notice, but they still asked us to come and see the pictures just in case a parent's eye might notice something they missed.

There was a table in a *tatami*-mat room, in a quiet back room of the station, and on the table was a thick file of photographs. All were of unidentified corpses that had been found throughout Japan, and the objects found near them. My husband and I looked through all the pictures of unidentified young women. The first year, I looked at each photo, and whenever I came across a woman with a round face like Megumi's, my heart would stop. The experience was so unbearably frightening that, from the following year, I looked only at the photos of the objects at the scene and asked my husband to go through the pictures of the remains.

After a few visits, one of the officers in charge suggested, "We are doing our best to find your daughter and I am sure that this is very painful for you. Please don't come if you would rather not."

It was a frightening and painful experience. Yet, my husband and I went to the police station each year, thinking that we might find something.

Whenever my husband or I walked along the street, we couldn't help but notice if there was a girl or young woman about Megumi's age. If we saw a picture in the newspaper of anyone who resembled Megumi, we would contact the publisher to ask about her, even though we knew in our hearts that she was not likely to be our daughter.

This happened several times. Once, it was a picture of a woman at a shrine on New Year's Day, making her first visit of the year. On the second occasion, it was a picture of a woman wearing an apron, standing with other people in a flower shop. Even standing among others, a woman who looked like Megumi caught our attention. When we explained the situation to the publishers, they kindly enlarged the photos and sent them to us. We pored over the pictures but the women were not Megumi.

We happened upon another such photo in the spring of 1989. In spite of my earlier disappointments, I again found the resemblance impossible to ignore.

My husband had been transferred to Maebashi after his posting in Tokyo. By this time, my husband and I were going out together occasionally for two or three hours. One day, we had gone to see an exhibition at a museum, and stopped at a noodle shop on our way home.

On the table in the shop was a locally published community magazine called *The Monthly Joshukko*. I was looking through it casually when I noticed an article with the title, "Finalists for the 1989 Miss Bowling Contest." It was a beauty contest sponsored by an association of bowling alleys, and the finalists were representing the Kanto area. Five women had been chosen to represent Gunma Prefecture, and there were not only pictures of their faces, but also pictures of them wearing street clothes and swimsuits.

One of the women among the finalists had a face and an air that really evoked Megumi.

Until then, my husband thought that I was seeing a resemblance to Megumi in every woman with a round face and hair cut like Megumi's, and often chided me for it. But this time, when I asked him, "Don't you think this young woman looks like her?" he nodded and said, "Yes, now that you point it out, it does look like her."

According to the article, the women were to appear in the finals, which was going to be held at Shinagawa Prince Hotel in Tokyo. The date was given, so I decided to go and see for myself.

The opening ceremony was scheduled to start at 10:15 in the morning. I arrived there 30 minutes early and took a seat in the center of the second row from the front, and waited for the young woman to appear. I was almost certain that I was wrong. But at the same time, I found myself wondering what sort of expression would cross her face if this was indeed Megumi and her eyes met mine. I looked toward the stage and waited.

When the woman appeared, I knew immediately that it wasn't Megumi. Her resemblance to Megumi was very strong, however, so I was struck by a sense of familiarity and found myself hoping that Megumi had grown up to look like her.

At the end of the contest, I introduced myself to one of the staff and asked if I could have a word with the young woman representing Gunma. I was told that I could not see her there, but I was given her telephone number. I called her at her home the next day, as soon as I returned to Maebashi.

It so happened that the young woman answered the telephone herself. I told her that I was looking for my daughter and that she looked so much like her that I had gone to Tokyo to see her in the contest and asked for her telephone number. The woman told me that she was very sorry, but she was born in Gunma. She also told me about her family. "Please, don't give up," she encouraged me before saying goodbye.

I went to such lengths to follow up every possibility. I couldn't help myself. I couldn't bear the thought of agonizing afterwards that it might have been Megumi.

A number of years ago, I encountered another face that resembled my daughter's. It was a girl in a portrait that I happened to see in 1994, some seventeen years after Megumi's disappearance.

We had moved to Kawasaki about three years before. One day, when I was looking at the local Kanagawa section of the newspaper, there was an article about a solo exhibition by a woman artist that was opening at a gallery in Kannai. The painting shown alongside the article was of a flower and a girl with almond-shaped eyes. With her straight hair, cut in a bob, and bangs cut straight across her forehead, the girl looked like a Japanese doll.

The more I looked at the portrait, the more it resembled Megumi. My husband had retired a year earlier, so the two of us immediately went to visit the gallery. When we looked at the actual portrait, even the expression on the girl's face resembled Megumi's.

The artist was a woman of about sixty. She happened to be at the gallery, so we explained to her that we were looking for our daughter. We explained that when we saw the painting in the newspaper, we decided to come on the chance that our daughter had perhaps become an amnesiac and somehow had come to model for the artist. The woman was very surprised and told us, "Unfortunately, the model in this portrait is a student of my daughter, who teaches tea ceremony." She added that she knew the woman's background as well.

Later, when it was reported in the press that Megumi had been abducted to North Korea, this artist wrote us a very kind letter. She wrote that she remembered our visit, and encouraged us to keep up our spirits. More than two years had passed since that visit, so we were both surprised and touched.

For twenty years, I couldn't stop inquiring after any woman that I thought resembled Megumi. The same impulse kept me from attending weddings, no matter how close I was to the person who invited me. I knew that I would think about Megumi when I looked at the bride, and that it would be unbearable for me.

My husband and I had done our best to raise our daughter. And yet, we were denied not only the pleasure of watching our daughter grow into adolescence and adulthood, but of seeing her as a bride on her wedding day, a day of pride and joy for a parent.

Was She Abducted to a Foreign Country?

If Megumi had vanished a hundred years ago, it would have been easy to understand the dearth of clues about her whereabouts. But this was modern-day Japan, an age of mass media and information overload. It was always puzzling that not a single lead could turn up in the disappearance of a young girl.

An adult can disappear; it would be possible, if one wished, to live elsewhere without being recognized. But a thirteen-year-old girl had no way of knowing how to live on her own. Even if she was involved in some kind of accident, it didn't happen in the middle of the mountains so it seemed impossible that nobody had seen anything.

Every day, we read the newspaper from front to back, looking for something that might give us a clue.

About two years after her disappearance, on January 7, 1980, a friend came by with a copy of the newspaper, *Sankei Shimbun*, to show me an article. The moment my husband and I read the paper, I instinctively thought, this might be it—this might be the explanation for everything. It was a huge front-page story with the following headline, readouts, and subheads: "Mysterious Disappearance of Three Couples from Beaches in Fukui, Niigata and Kagoshima in the Summer of 1978," "Failed kidnapping attempt in Toyama spurs National Police Agency to investigate," "Involvement by a foreign intelligence agency?" "Same group suspected in all incidents; foreign-made objects left at scene," and "Possible motive: to acquire domicile registry?" There was a detailed report on the disappearance of the three couples, along with their pictures.

We were later to learn that the article was written by Masami Abe, a *Sankei Shimbun* journalist in the City News department. (He is now Associate Managing Editor and head of City News at the paper's Osaka Branch Office). He was the first to report that there was "strong evidence to suggest the involvement of a foreign intelligence agency" in the series of disappearances taking place along the coast of the Sea of Japan.

Further details of the mysterious disappearances appeared in the issues published on January 8 and 9.

The three young couples had all vanished in July and August, 1978, the year after Megumi's disappearance. Those missing were Yasushi Chimura and Fukie Hamamoto of Obama City in Fukui Prefecture, Shuichi Ichikawa and Rumiko Masumoto of Hioki District, Kagoshima Prefecture, and a third-year student at Chuo University and a beautician, both from Kashiwazaki City, Niigata Prefecture. We later learned that the Chuo University student not named in the article was Kaoru Hasuike and the beautician was Yukiko Okudo, who worked as a make-up adviser at a cosmetics company. All of them were in their twenties.

I will write of this later in greater detail, but my husband and I, along with the parents and siblings of those who disappeared, formed a group in March 1997 called "The Association of the Families of Victims Kidnapped by North Korea," and my husband became the chairperson of the group.

To get back to the article published on January 7, 1980, the story began with this lead:

The National Police Agency has identified six people as missing in a succession of mysterious disappearances of couples from coastal areas near the Sea of Japan. Three separate couples disappeared from the prefectures of Fukui, Niigata and Kagoshima, but a possible connection came to light after an attempted kidnapping in Toyama.

The National Police Agency announced on [January] 6th that it believes a single group is responsible for the series of disappearances and the botched kidnapping attempt. The incidents took place over a wide area but appear to have been carefully planned. Furthermore, the incidents took place within a time span of forty days in the summer of 1978.

Objects left behind in Toyama by the would-be kidnappers were all foreign-made and impossible to acquire domestically. Many suspicious radio communications that could be espionage-related were intercepted at the time in the areas where these disappearances occurred. Based on these circumstances, there is strong suspicion of involvement by a foreign intelligence agency.

The kidnapping attempt that alerted the officials regarding the other disappearances involved a couple living in Takaoka City in Toyama Prefecture. The couple, who were engaged to be married, had gone swimming at Shimao Beach on the coast of the Sea of Japan. After their swim they were almost kidnapped by a suspicious group of four men. This couple was also in their twenties.

They had gone to the beach with other relatives. The relatives, considerate of the couple's privacy, had left ahead, at around five o'clock. The couple swam a little longer and then, at around six thirty, they were rushed by four men as they were walking up the beach.

The four men had come from the opposite direction, but instead of walking past they suddenly wrestled the two to the ground. They handcuffed the young man's hands behind his back, tied his feet together, put a towel in his mouth and placed some kind of special gag on him before dropping a cloth hood over his head. They also tied the woman's hands behind her back, put a gag on her, and placed a cloth hood over her head as well.

The four picked up the couple and carried them to a nearby stand of pine trees where they rolled them onto the ground and covered them with pine branches to keep them hidden. According to the article,. "They carried out the attack in a very business-like way. They were quick and each knew what he was supposed to do." The article goes on to add, "The four sat with the victims in front of them and seemed to be waiting for something."

During the wait, the couple never heard the four speak among themselves, and only once, one of them told the woman to be quiet. About thirty minutes later, a dog barked nearby, and the four men disappeared. The man hopped, still bound and with the hood over his head, to a house approximately a hundred meters away and sought help.

The couple recalls that the four men all wore long loose pants, short-sleeve shirts and running shoes. They were in their mid-thirties, and all were muscular and darkly tanned.

When I read this article, I thought that if two grown people could be taken away like this, it would have been easy for a few men to abduct a thirteen-year-old.

The summer seas are calm while the sea in November, when Megumi disappeared, is rougher. The victims in the other disappearances were in their twenties and included men. But despite these differences, there were circumstances similar to Megumi's. They all disappeared in the evening or early in the night; the university student and his girlfriend disappeared from Kashiwazaki City, which is also in Niigata Prefecture. Massive searches were conducted for all of them in case they had drowned, but no bodies were ever found.

When I had finished reading the article, I took the newspaper to the Niigata bureau of the *Sankei Shimbun* that very day and told the bureau chief that I was searching for my own daughter. Since there were no clues to explain her disappearance, I told him that I thought my daughter might have met a fate similar to the couples in the article, and asked for his opinion.

The bureau chief thought for a while then said, "Your daughter is not in the same age range as the others. Also, these disappearances all involve couples." He gently added, "Don't you think the circumstances are a little different?"

That morning, I had talked to my husband about the newspaper article and my husband shared the same opinion as the bureau chief. The article surmised that the young people had been kidnapped in order to acquire their domicile registries* for espionage-related activities. If we supposed that the article was correct, and the young people had been kidnapped for the registries required to apply for Japanese passports, Megumi was too young. Because she was only thirteen

---

* An important proof of registration required as personal identification when applying for a driver's license or passport.

years old, it would have been impossible to get her passport without our signatures. We had very little knowledge of North Korea at the time, so my husband concluded that common sense ruled out any connection between Megumi's disappearance and the missing couples.

After leaving the newspaper bureau, I went to the Niigata Police Central Station and repeated my theory. The police also were of the opinion that Megumi's disappearance was unrelated to the others, based on her age and other discrepancies.

I went home dispirited. I thought that I had a possible explanation for Megumi's disappearance, but that it had been refuted.

Of course I had no way of knowing at the time that the "foreign intelligence agency" referred to in the article could be North Korean spies. It was just intuition on my part that the disappearances were all related, for the serial disappearances were as unexpected and inexplicable as Megumi's.

I had little knowledge at the time of North Korea, and it was only after I learned of Megumi's true whereabouts that I began to give it any thought. But looking back, there were times when we felt flickers of North Korea's shadow lurking near us in Niigata.

Megumi's disappearance took place only a year and three months after we moved to Niigata, so we had not yet become familiar with the area. But an acquaintance who had lived for a long time in Niigata once let slip the comment, "This may be something that the police can't solve." At the time, I did not know what this friend was taking about. And since my husband and I had complete confidence in the police, I simply assured our friend, "We've left everything in the hands of the police." Recalling those words now, it seems to me that my friend might have been referring to North Korea. Even so, it is unlikely that our friend had any real basis for making those comments.

Shortly before we left Niigata, a particularly vicious rumor about Megumi began circulating, again involving North Korea. The rumor was that Megumi had been taken to North Korea but had gone insane and been returned and was now hospitalized at a mental institution in Niigata City.

I found out about this rumor by chance. When I was shopping at a department store in Niigata, I met the mother of my children's friend. She came running to me and said, "I am so glad they found Megumi!" Surprised, I asked her, "Where is she?" She was equally surprised at my response and said, "Did I say something wrong? I am sorry if I said anything that hurt you." That was how I learned about the rumor.

Of course, Megumi had not returned. I tried to trace the rumor, but never discovered the source. It was too cruel to be a joke. Anyone who actually believed the rumor would have hesitated to inform the authorities even if they spotted Megumi somewhere.

My husband and I were starved for any kind of information. Yet, more often than not, we were pained and frustrated by the lack of real information and the proliferation of talk by the idle and curious.

When we found out about this rumor, my husband and I went to the police and asked them to announce that any rumor that Megumi had returned was a lie. The police sympathized and made an announcement that Megumi's investigation was still ongoing. The newspapers carried an article under the headline, "Cruel Rumors Deepen Family's Sorrow."

I still don't know how that rumor was started, but it continues to worry me because of a puzzling coincidence: I later learned that a former North Korean agent had testified that Megumi had suffered a mental breakdown and was hospitalized. The testimony was given at about the same time that the rumor began to circulate.

Geographically, Niigata is close to the Korean Peninsula. The North Korean ship *Man Gyon Bong* often docked at the central port in Niigata. There is no denying that North Korea has had frequent contact with Japan, but all this knowledge came to us later. At the time, it was inconceivable that Megumi could have been taken to North Korea.

Reverend McDaniel

Shortly after the investigation for Megumi became public, I met an American minister, the Reverend McDaniel. He and his wife were Christian mission-aries who lived in our neighborhood. He came to my house with a stack of homemade flyers on which he had copied a picture of Megumi from a newspaper and written a description of what had taken place. He suggested that we go to the Niigata port together to hand out the flyers.

I was still deep in shock and had no desire to go out, so I had him take my two young sons instead. At the time, a large Russian ship was in port and I heard that the Reverend boarded the ship and handed out his flyers to the crewmen on board.

I wonder why it had occurred to the Reverend to go to the port as his first course of action. As I look back, it seems a curious thing to do. Perhaps during his thirty years in Niigata a missing person had been traced through information obtained at the port.

It seems to me that the people of Niigata have an instinctive fear of the port because of the unknown dangers that can enter through it. This didn't occur to me right away because I grew up inland, near Nijo Castle in Kyoto. When I was small and was late coming home, I remember being warned that "a child snatcher will come and sell you to a circus." But I have heard from people who grew up near ports that if a child got lost, its parents worry that the child had been put on a ship and taken to a foreign country. Perhaps this possibility had crossed Reverend McDaniel's mind as well.

In any case, this was the beginning of my friendship with Rev. McDaniel. We have now known each other for over twenty years.

After her disappearance, I did everything possible to find Megumi. Yet, a month, three months, half a year, then a year slipped by and I had no knowledge of what had happened to her. Time moved forward, but I could not; my heart felt weighed down by loneliness and despair. I tried to keep my hopes up, telling myself, "Today, I will hear her voice, as full of energy as ever. Tomorrow I will surely see her smiling, standing in my doorway." But after my husband and sons left for work and school, I would succumb to waves of grief.

At the first sign of winter, when large snowflakes begin to fall in Niigata, I would gaze outside the window and wonder where my child could be in such bitter weather. Then the tears would start and I would be powerless to help myself.

I wanted to die. I couldn't understand how so much unhappiness could be thrust upon me. How could I rise up above my grief? I cried endlessly, I tried to stop breathing, I went to the beach and tried to focus on the thought of death, and yet every day a new, yet still sad, morning arrived.

At that time, many people came to my house to share their religious beliefs. Some of their words stabbed my heart like knives. "A child is a mirror of his parents. The child reflects everything that is in the parent." Or, "What goes around, comes around. These things making headlines in the newspapers are retribution for the actions of your ancestors." When I heard those words, I thought of my ancestors and cried for my parents, who had lived honest lives, true to themselves and to others.

At the risk of sounding immodest, I would describe my parents as people who taught me sound values from the time I was a very small child. They told me time and again that one must live within one's means and avoid being wasteful, that one must be self-reliant and speak with conviction against wrongdoing and injustice. I have tried to be true to my parents' teachings and to live a principled life.

An acquaintance once urged, "When my child was lost, I asked a soothsayer to offer prayers for me, and she was found immediately." We went to see this person too, for my husband and I were ready to grasp at straws. But of course, there was no way my missing daughter could be found through such means, and I became more despondent than ever.

One day, when I was still deep in depression, a woman whose daughter was in the same grade as Megumi came to my house. She explained that she belonged to a Bible study group that met once a week at Reverend McDaniel's home nearby. "Why don't you come and join us?" she urged. And she left with me a big, thick Bible. She recommended that I read the Book of Job in particular. When I heard Reverend McDaniel's name, I recalled that he was the man who had gone to pass out leaflets at the port.

I opened the Bible, but in my state of mind I didn't think that I could read such a thick book packed with tiny print. I was alone, though; all I did was stare at the ceiling and feel the tears run down my face. I picked up the Bible and listlessly leafed through the pages. I remembered that my friend had recommended the Book of Job, so I opened to that section. It was the first time I had ever read the Bible.

In the Bible was written:

Naked I came from my mother's womb, and naked shall I return; the Lord gave, and the Lord has taken away; blessed be the name of the Lord. (Job 1:21)

I was struck by the words "The Lord gave, and the Lord has taken away." I, too, had given thought to the meaning of birth and death, both of which are inevitable for human beings. However, these words seemed to be telling me that there was a greater power involved in our birth and death.

Can you find out the deep things of God? Can you find out the limit of the Almighty? It is higher than heaven—what can you do? Deeper than Sheol—what can you know? (Job 11: 7-8)

These words, too, settled comfortably within me.

Encouraged, I went on to read the Book of Psalms, Epistle to the Romans, Epistle to the Corinthians, and the Book of Isaiah, one after the other. Every word eased my heart, for they were words that knew of pain. But I also came to see how self-righteous I had been. I cannot describe it very well, but I came to realize what an infinitely small creature I was to feel complacent just because I had tried to live a principled life.

The presence of God is beyond the measure of man. God knows all of the sadness and pain in this world. Because a human being is a small creature, the pain in my life and in Megumi's life is beyond what we can influence or even fathom. The Bible seemed to speak to me with this message.

I began to go to the Bible study meetings, and on Sundays, I went to Reverend McDaniel's church for the worship service.

In May 1984, I was baptized by Reverend McDaniel. I had studied the Bible and my baptism was my own decision. It was an action I took at a time in my life when I could do nothing but wait. At the same time, it was clear to me that the blessing of baptism was a gift from God, not deserved or earned, but a sign of God's grace.

Many times, my husband and I have thought that Megumi might never come back. Yet, just as we had no way of knowing if something had ended her life, we also had no proof that she wouldn't come back. So, we had no other choice but to believe that Megumi was alive. Words cannot describe how difficult it is to simply believe and wait, to stave off doubt every minute of our waking lives. After I was baptized, I was relieved of this emotional burden, for I had come to believe that everything is in God's hands.

It so happened that the year I received my baptism was the year Megumi turned twenty, the age of majority in Japan.

Through spiritual growth, I managed not to lose myself. Of course, I am not always serene; I experience great emotional turmoil from time to time. However, I can say now that my faith has made it possible for me to accept whatever is going to come at the end of my wait. I know that when death comes, as it does to everyone, my soul will be allowed at last to meet Megumi's, and then we will be together in peace.

Reverend McDaniel came to Sasebo as a soldier at the end of the war. He was deeply shocked by the devastation he witnessed in Nagasaki and other places in Japan, and he came to the conclusion that the origins of that tragic war were rooted in matters of the heart and spirit. This set him on his path and he became a Protestant missionary spreading God's teachings in Japan.

After thirty years of missionary work in Japan, Reverend and Mrs. McDaniel returned to the United States in 1986. He was a very important person in my life, so his departure made me feel very lonely at the time. Still, on my birthday, my husband's birthday, and on November 15, the date of Megumi's disappearance, the Reverend always calls us and never fails to give us fresh courage.

In 1995, I visited Reverend and Mrs. McDaniel in Philadelphia with four other friends from church. He was over eighty years old but still in good health. At his insistence, I went to three churches and senior centers to talk about my daughter, who by then had been missing for almost two decades. When I finished, many in my audience were in tears. They hugged me and told me that they would also pray for Megumi.

For these twenty years, since my first meeting with Reverend McDaniel, my daily prayer has been, "Dear God, if my daughter is still alive, please protect her, her life, her soul, and her health, from all harm."

My husband does not believe in any religion. I think this is because he believes that, as a father, he must remain strong. He has said that if Megumi is somewhere, bearing her pain alone, then he must also bear his pain of waiting for Megumi, alone. He has told me that he wishes to wait for Megumi's return without leaning on anything for support. I can feel the fierce inner strength that has supported my husband—a strength that is different from my own as a mother—and I have deep respect for his fortitude. But at the same time, I hope that one day my husband and I can pray together with one heart for our daughter.

Each in our own way, my husband and I withstood the difficulties of these two decades. When I heard in January 1997 that Megumi was in North Korea, a new ordeal began. This time, I had these words from the Book of Psalms to support me:

> Lord, my heart is not lifted up, my eyes are not raised too high; I do not occupy myself with things too great and too marvelous for me. But I have calmed and quieted my soul, like a child quieted at its mother's breast; like a child that is quieted is my soul. (Psalms 131:1-2)

For God alone my soul waits in silence; from him comes my salvation. (Psalms 62:1)

Trust in him at all times, O people; pour out your heart before him; God is a refuge for us. (Psalms 62:8)

Chapter IV
MEGUMI'S DIMPLE

Your Daughter Is Alive in North Korea

On January 21, 1997, I returned home from an afternoon prayer meeting at around six o'clock. My husband, now retired, was home and he greeted me with a strange expression on his face. He said, "Something strange happened today."

"What happened?" I asked. My husband didn't answer right away and when he did, he spoke haltingly.

"It's a really perplexing story."

"What is it? Tell me."

"Well, I don't know how to tell you this."

It was so unlike him that I instinctively deduced what it was about. "It's about Megumi, isn't it?"

My husband replied that it was, and related a most surprising and extraordinary story.

That day, just around lunch, he had received a call from the Friends of BOJ Club, a group similar to an alumni association, whose members are former officials of the Bank of Japan. The club had received a call from Tatsukichi Hyomoto, the personal secretary to Atsushi Hashimoto, a member of the Japanese Communist Party who had been elected to the House of Councilors. Mr. Hyomoto had requested that my husband get in touch with him.

The Friends of BOJ Club had no further details to relate, so my husband, completely mystified, immediately phoned Mr. Hyomoto.

He was surprised beyond words when Mr. Hyomoto told him over the phone, "We have information that your daughter is alive in North Korea." He went on to explain that he had been investigating abductions of Japanese by North Korea. Our daughter's disappearance had been brought to his attention only recently and he wished to know about it in greater detail.

Mr. Hyomoto preferred not to discuss the matter over the phone and asked my husband if he would come to the Diet Members' Building. My husband promised that he would be there directly and hurried to see him.

My husband told me that, on his way to the Diet Members' Building, he could think of only two things. First, this was the first piece of substantial information we had received regarding Megumi, but he wasn't sure how credible it was. Second, if this information was accurate, how could he bring Megumi back from North Korea? My husband felt quite anxious as he rode the train to the meeting.

Mr. Hyomoto was waiting for him with the October 1996 issue of a magazine published by the Modern Korea Institute as well as a copy of the newspaper article reporting Megumi's disappearance that had appeared twenty years ago in the *Niigata Nippo*.

We would later learn that, during the Upper House Budget Committee meeting of March 26, 1988, Councilor Hashimoto had asked questions regarding the three couples who had disappeared mysteriously in the summer of 1978. My husband later acquired a copy of the minutes of this meeting (Volume 15 of the Minutes of the 112th Session of the Upper House Budget Committee) and among the members who had replied to Councilor Hashimoto's questions was Seiroku Kajiyama, then Chairman of the National Public Safety Commission. According to the minutes, Mr. Kajiyama had said:

> There is strong evidence to suggest that the series of mysterious disappearances that have taken place since 1978 is the result of abductions instigated by North Korea. It is extremely difficult to verify the truth of the matter, but taking into consideration the seriousness of the incidents, I think that we must do everything possible to investigate the facts. At the same time, I would like to express my deep sympathy, not only to those who were abducted, but to their families.

The Foreign Minister at the time was the late Sousuke Uno. He made the following comment:

> I am of the same opinion as the Chairman of the National Public Safety Commission [Seiroku Kajiyama]. As I have stated before, in this age of peace and modern statehood, this is a serious issue that severely compromises our country's sovereign rights. And if there is the slightest truth to these allegations, it is at the same time an unforgivable infringement of individual rights on humanitarian grounds, and I feel deep anger over these actions.

I am quoting at length here, but I would like to mention one other person who responded at the above committee meeting, the Head of the Guard Division of the National Police Agency, Yasumitsu Jyonai:

> This series of incidents strongly suggests abduction by the North Koreans. We have already launched an investigation to pursue this angle.

I had been right in January 1980, after reading the article in the *Sankei Shimbun* newspaper, when I speculated that Megumi might have been abducted in the same manner as those three couples. My husband and I were both surprised, however, that at least so far as the disappearance of the young couples were concerned, the issue had been discussed at the Diet some ten years ago and it was already recognized at the time that North Korea was implicated. It is no use for us to bemoan the delay at this late stage, and I know that we must take into consideration the fact that it is a difficult investigation, but I cannot help but wish that we had known the truth earlier.

To return to the meeting between my husband and Mr. Hyomoto on January 21, Mr. Hyomoto told my husband that he had received a fax of the magazine *Modern Korea* and the article in *Niigata Nippo* from an acquaintance. The acquaintance had attached a memo reading, "Please read. The abducted middle school girl was Megumi Yokota." Mr. Hyomoto learned from reading *Niigata Nippo* that my husband had worked at the Bank of Japan, so he had contacted the Friends of BOJ Club in order to get in touch with us.

We had a copy of the *Niigata Nippo* at home of course, but it was the first time my husband had seen the magazine published by the Modern Korea Institute. Mr. Hyomoto directed his attention to an article by Kenji Ishidaka titled "Why I Wrote *Kim Jong Il's Abduction Orders*." (The book was published by Asahi Shimbun Publishing. A revised paperback edition was published for the Asahi Paperback series in 1998.)

Kenji Ishidaka was a program director for Asahi Broadcasting Corporation who produced a television documentary on the abductions of Japanese citizens by North Korea. (Based in Osaka at the time, he is now Chief of News Center of his company's Tokyo bureau.) He wrote his book based on material he gathered while producing the documentary, including information provided by high-ranking officials in South Korea's Agency for National Security Planning (NSP—South Korea's intelligence agency).* His article in *Modern Korea* was based on statements made by these officials, whom he interviewed in 1995.

My husband showed me a copy of the article in *Modern Korea*, which Mr. Hyomoto had given him earlier that day. Mr. Ishidaka began his article by stating that he had been unable to include the interviews in his book because he lacked sufficient information to corroborate the NSP officials' words. But he shares some of their claims as follows:

> I write this with the hope that anyone who has any information will contact me because this particular abduction was particularly appalling and cruel: the victim was a child.
>
> This incident came to light in late 1994, in testimony by a North Korean spy who had defected to South Korea. According to this former agent, a year or two before the abductions of couples along the Sea of Japan, perhaps in 1976 [in fact, it was 1977], a thirteen-year-old girl was also abducted to North Korea from the Sea of Japan coast. The former agent did not know at which beach this abduction took place. The girl was on her way home from school after badminton practice. The girl happened to see North Korean spies on the

---

* The Agency is now known as the National Intelligence Service.

verge of departing via the beach, so they abducted her and took her back to North Korea.

The girl was very intelligent and studied diligently because she was told, "If you learn Korean, we will take you back to your mother." When she was about eighteen years old, she realized that she would never be able to return home, and suffered a mental breakdown. The former agent learned of these facts while the girl was in the hospital. He heard that the girl was the younger of a pair of twins.

My husband told me that as soon as he read this article, he was sure that the girl was Megumi. The fact that the girl was "thirteen years old" and was "on her way home from badminton practice" convinced him. Though she is the older sister of twins, rather than the younger of a set of twins herself, it is true that we have twin children and only people who knew us personally knew of Megumi's younger brothers.

Mr. Ishidaka told us later that he had heard the story of "the thirteen-year-old girl kidnapped from Japan" from a number of top officials in the NSP who had been present during the interrogation of the former agent. So, it seems reasonable to assume that it may have been in recounting the agent's testimony that the information changed from "the girl has twin siblings younger than she" to "the girl is the younger of a set of twins."

My husband's instincts told him that this girl was Megumi. At the same time, however, his intellect told

him that it was entirely possible to make up a story
like this based on the reports written in newspapers
immediately after Megumi's disappearance. As a matter
of fact, the high school student who made the phony
kidnapping call had fabricated his story based on the
knowledge he gained from newspapers and television
reports after the investigation was made public. And I
had believed him.

If this recent story could be corroborated by facts
known only to the family, for instance, a place our
family had been to on a vacation, or the dates, then we
could confirm that the girl was Megumi. But because
there was no conclusive evidence at the time, my
husband had come home quite perplexed.

When I heard my husband's story, my heart beat
faster and my spine tingled. I was elated at first. "She's
alive. What joy!" Then, slowly, my excitement subsided
and doubt began to set in. Is it possible for this kind of
truth to emerge after twenty years? Why did the spies
have to take Megumi with them, back to North Korea?
Half of me wanted to believe, but the other half was in
doubt, and I became confused.

So often, my husband and I had raised our hopes
only to be bitterly disappointed. This had happened so
many times before that we were now cautious. Either
nothing would corroborate Mr. Ishidaka's story and we
would never know more, or we would have to wait for
the next development.

This time, there was more, and the decisive
factor was Mr. Ishidaka's article. It set many things in

motion, and at last there appeared a man who gave solid testimony that Megumi was indeed in North Korea.

Should We Use Our Real Names?

There are two dates I will never forget: November 15, 1977, the day Megumi disappeared, and January 21, 1997, the day my husband was first contacted regarding the North Korean kidnappings. These two dates turned the tide of our life. The news that Megumi was in North Korea was like a thunderbolt out of a blue sky. For us, this is neither an exaggeration nor a worn-out expression. The weeks that followed felt as though we had suddenly been tossed into the center of a storm.

For twenty years, we hadn't had a single clue that could help us to find Megumi. The reality for our family was that, despite our grief, we had to live on. And I decided that we could do so only by leaving everything in God's hands, and praying for my daughter. I tried to live day to day, focusing on what I could do—bringing up my sons the best I could, and looking after the well-being of my family.

It was when I finally thought that I was developing some forbearance that this tremendous piece of information sprang out at me.

Thrown as we were into a maelstrom, my husband and I were not able to understand the significance of each new piece of information as we encountered it. But my husband, always a meticulous person, kept a memo of all that happened. Based on his notes and what we learned later, I would like to relate how we came to believe with certainty that Megumi was in North Korea.

Modern Korea, the magazine that printed Mr. Ishidaka's article, is published by the Modern Korea Institute. The head of the institute is Katsumi Sato, who happens to be from Niigata. When he read Mr. Ishidaka's article for the October edition of his magazine, a vague memory stirred in the back of his mind.

Two months after publication of the October edition, on December 14, 1996, Mr. Sato had the occasion to speak in Niigata City. At a reception following his presentation, Mr. Sato asked those around him about the girl who had disappeared from the coast of Niigata. A top official of the Niigata Prefectural Police Department who was there responded, "Oh, yes. You must be referring to Megumi." When Mr. Sato told him, "I understand that she is in North Korea," his words were greeted with amazement and consternation.

Mr. Sato immediately obtained a copy of the *Niigata Nippo* article, and the Modern Korea Institute asked authorities in South Korea to verify the testimony by the officials of the Agency for National Security Planning as it appeared in Mr. Ishidaka's article. The NSP confirmed that its officials had been quoted correctly.

The Modern Korea Institute decided that the girl was indeed our daughter and published an article in the January/February 1997 edition of *Modern Korea* with

the headline, "Identity of Abducted Girl Confirmed."
At the same time, the Institute sent word out to the
media through its website. The Institute also consulted
with Shingo Nishimura, a member of the New Frontier
Party (renamed the Liberal Party) elected to the Lower
House. Mr. Nishimura promised to pursue the matter
in the Diet. Many people had begun to work on our
behalf before we even knew.

On January 23, Representative Nishimura
initiated formal proceedings with the government,
submitting a Letter of Inquiry and Intent on the
Subject of the Abduction of Japanese People by North
Korean Agents. We learned of this five days later, on
January 28.

Mr. Ishidaka, who had written the *Modern Korea*
article that set all of these events in motion, visited
us on the 23rd and 25th to brief us. On the 25th, we
were interviewed by Hiroshi Hasegawa, a journalist
for the weekly magazine *Aera* (published by Asahi
Shimbun). We were interviewed on the 28th by Hideko
Takayama for a *Newsweek* (Japanese edition) piece, and
Masami Abe of the *Sankei Shimbun* also came to our
house. *Sankei Shimbun* was the newspaper that first
wrote of the mysterious serial disappearances of young
couples back in 1980. We also learned that day that
Representative Nishimura had submitted a Letter of
Inquiry on the 23rd.

Upon learning of the Letter of Inquiry, my husband phoned Representative Nishimura the following
day, the 29th. Representative Nishimura informed us

that the government was not ready to respond right away. It was not until February 7 that we received a response, which was: "The status of the Megumi Yokota incident is 'still under investigation.'"

On January 30, my husband and I visited the Niigata Police Central Station to inform them of the recent developments. Afterwards, we went to the lot where our house had stood, and I saw the camellia that had grown into a tall tree in my neighbor's garden. The house where our family of five had spent such a happy time had been torn down and was now a vacant lot full of weeds. All that was left was the gate with the lattice, and the plum tree that had been planted by the front door.

I didn't like looking at the street corner where Megumi had disappeared, let alone going to stand on the very spot. It was unbearable for me to think that Megumi had vanished there. If she hadn't been abducted, she would have turned that corner and walked just a short distance to return safely home. She probably would have fussed a little about the pressure of having been chosen for the special training program, and I probably would have wondered if I should speak to the coach about it. My biggest concern would have been, "What should a parent do in such a situation?"

But no. What happened, happened, and I now had other worries. After we returned from Niigata on January 31, Mr. Hasegawa of Asahi Shimbun, the publisher of *Aera*, came to our house again with a sample copy featuring a cover story on Megumi's disappearance. This issue of *Aera* was to appear on newsstands two days later, and Mr. Hasegawa had come to ask our permission to identify us in the article by our real names.

When Mr. Hasegawa told us that he would like to print our names, so many thoughts raced through my mind that I thought I would go insane. Since we had no real evidence regarding Megumi's disappearance at that time, I wondered what kind of repercussions there would be if we allowed *Aera* to reveal our identities. If Megumi were indeed alive and living in North Korea, I thought about the possible impact on her life. I feared that Megumi might be killed in order to cover up evidence. If that happened, I would never be able to live with myself. What were we to do? Could we have them delay the publication of *Aera*? I desperately wanted more time to think about it.

I phoned my sons, both of whom lived far away, to discuss this matter. I told them that their father and I were of different opinions. My sons thought that their father was right, but that he wasn't thinking as a father. Even if it delayed the resolution of the matter, they were against anything that might heighten the risk to Megumi. They agreed with me that we should not allow our names to appear in print.

My husband alone thought that we should allow our names to appear. His logic was that, for twenty years, there had been no change in our situation because of the lack of real information. If the article were published using assumed names or references to

"Miss Y.M."—as is often done—it would lose much of its credibility. Megumi's abduction would be a subject in conversations for a short time, then disappear from people's memories. If that happened, our present situation might continue for twenty more years; by then we may no longer be alive.

He weighed the risks but thought that we should allow our names to appear, thus making a public appeal regarding our plight. He also thought that using our names would send a clear message to North Korea: Japan has a lot of information about your activities; harming Megumi will bring grave repercussions. My husband thought that it might actually help protect Megumi. Also, the Modern Korea Institute's website had already disclosed the real nature of Megumi's disappearance using her full name. He determined that we should allow Asahi to publish our names in the *Aera* article.

I worried through the night trying to reach a decision, but in the end, I decided to trust my husband's judgment and agreed.

The February 10 edition of the magazine, *Aera*, went on the newsstands on February 3. The *Sankei Shimbun* newspaper also published an article on both its first page and the city news page that Megumi had been abducted to North Korea. The article also included her picture. The headline was, "North Korean Spy Testifies to Kidnapping Thirteen-Year-Old Girl," and the sub-heads and headlines of related articles read: "Extraordinary Similarity to Serial Disappearances in Niigata," "Information from South Korea,"

"Badminton, twins—parents say, 'We think this is our daughter,'" and "Megumi's parents continued search, did not declare her dead."

That same day, Representative Nishimura asked about the abduction during the Lower House Budget Committee meeting and Ryutaro Hashimoto, then Prime Minister, replied that it was "still under investigation."

Later that year, on May 1, Yoshio Yoshikawa, a Liberal Democratic Party member of the House of Councilors, brought the matter up again at the Upper House Budget Committee meeting. For the first time, the government publicly acknowledged that it believes the disappearances to be abductions instigated by North Korea. According to newspaper reports, the government also revised its official estimate of the number of victims kidnapped to North Korea: from the initial "nine people in six separate incidents" to "seven incidents totaling ten people." The revised figures also appeared in the National Police White Paper of 1997. Although neither provided names, I believe that Megumi was recognized at this point as the tenth victim.

Shortly after noon on February 3, the day Representative Nishimura posed his question at the Budget Committee meeting, a journalist on his way to South Korea to research a story happened to see the headlines of *Aera* and *Sankei Shimbun* at the Narita Airport bookstore. He was surprised at the number of pages devoted to Megumi's disappearance and purchased both copies. The journalist was Hitoshi Takase, head of the News Center at Nihon Denpa News Company. Because he happened to see these articles on the newsstand and bought them, we were to hear our first direct testimony of what had happened to Megumi and her whereabouts. The testimony came from a former North Korean agent, An Myon Jin, in an interview conducted by Mr. Takase.

Testimony from a Former Spy

Mr. Takase and his crew of reporters had been investigating a story that started with the discovery of counterfeit US dollars being circulated in Thailand. They were on their way to South Korea to interview a former North Korean agent in relation to this story, and Mr. Takase had noticed the *Aera* and *Sankei Shimbun* articles just before boarding his flight to Seoul. He writes of this trip in his book, *Give Us Back Our Sons and Daughters*, published by Junposha in April 1999:

> Toward the end of March 1996, a man was taken into custody at the border between Cambodia and Vietnam and charged with using counterfeit American dollars in Thailand. The man turned out to be Yoshimi Tanaka, a member of the Japanese Red Army and a suspect in the 1970 hijacking of a Japan Airlines flight, which was forced at gunpoint to fly to North Korea (known

in Japan as the "Yodo Incident"). Hearing this news, we immediately started our investigation and produced a documentary report that aired on the Asahi television program *Sunday Project*.

In January 1997, we interviewed An Myon Jin, a former North Korean agent, in relation to this counterfeiting bust. I had met him for the first time on October 1, 1996. The previous month, a North Korean submarine had drifted ashore on the outskirts of Kangnung, a city on the eastern coast of South Korea, and the crew had tried to flee into the mountains. I interviewed An about this incident in order to get a better understanding of North Korean espionage activities. He had been a spy until September 1993, when he crossed the 38th parallel and secretly entered South Korea, where he sought political asylum.

As I chatted with An at the end of our first interview, he mentioned something that surprised us, information of a nature that contrasted starkly with the casual tone of his disclosure. He said that he had seen a member of the Japanese Red Army in North Korea.

Prior to this interview, our reports on the counterfeiting arrest of a Japanese Red Army member in Thailand had already aired in Japan. The Korean Broadcasting System (KBS) had asked for the video material used in this report and produced their own program using the material. An had seen this program and recognized the faces of people he had seen in North Korea.

What we found troubling was that An had seen the member of the Japanese Red Army at Kim Jong Il Political and Military University, a kind of training school for spies that was under the direct supervision of the Central Committee of the Workers' Party. We asked the Korean authorities in January 1997 for permission to interview An once more. We wished to focus on this new angle in relation to the counterfeit dollar bust.

For this interview, we had sought permission from the Agency for National Security Planning to interview four defectors, including An Myon Jin. The NSP's permission is necessary for anyone to interview a defector, although the department cannot force any defector to be interviewed. Only if the defector agrees to the interview does the NSP proceed to work out a schedule. Toward the end of January, we received word that all four defectors had agreed to be interviewed. The dates were February 4 and 5, one interview in the morning and another in the afternoon of each day. An was our second interviewee and was scheduled for the afternoon of the 4th.

Mr. Takase had read of Megumi on the Modern Korea Institute website but says that, to his great embarrassment he didn't make the connection and the only thought that entered his head was, "I wouldn't put it past the North Koreans to do something like this."

But at the airport, he was surprised at the extent of coverage in *Aera* and *Sankei Shimbun*, and decided that he would ask about Megumi's abduction during his interview on the counterfeit money story.

It was NSP policy for an official from the department to be present during interviews, and for all questions to be submitted to them in advance. Mr. Takase had to request permission to ask about Megumi, since the question was not on the list he had submitted. Receiving permission, he showed An Myon Jin a picture of Megumi and explained that North Korea was suspected of having abducted her. He asked An if he knew anything about her.

An stared at the picture for a time, then said slowly, "I remember seeing her." Surprised, Mr. Takase inquired further.

On the evening of February 6, Mr. Takase showed my husband and me the unedited video of the interview and told us in detail about Mr. An's testimony.

From 1988 to 1991, Mr. An was a student at Kim Jong Il Political and Military University, the training school for spies. He said that he had seen a woman who resembled Megumi several times while he was a student there. According to Mr. An, she looked to be about 25 to 27 years old. Megumi would have been 24 or 25 at the time, so the age is about right.

Mr. An first saw the woman in October 1988. His testimony appears in Mr. Takase's book as follows:

At Kim Jong Il University, students and staff

gather at a great hall on important commem-
orative days. There were about ten Japanese staff
and three of them were women. I think that it
was on October 10, 1988 when we commemorated
the founding of the North Korean Workers' Party.
As I sat near the front row in the center waiting
for the ceremony to begin, one of our instructors
told us that the woman (who looked like Megumi)
was a girl he had brought over from Japan. When
we turned our heads to look behind us, a woman
came in and sat in the rows to the right, about
midway from the stage. The Japanese staff is
always the last to come into the hall and on that
day, this woman was the last of the staff to enter.
She was the girl in this picture.

Mr. An did not reveal the full name of his
instructor but said that his last name was Chon. Chon
was many years older than An, and he told An that when
he infiltrated Japan in the seventies, he had brought the
young woman to North Korea. Mr. Takase's account goes
on to say that the spies in training at the university were
all young men and they became interested in the young
woman, peppering their instructor with questions. As
the young woman resembling Megumi was pretty, the
young spies wondered among themselves if she were
married.

Listening to Mr. Takase's video, we could hear the
words "Niigata" sprinkling the conversation conducted
in Korean. At that time, we were not acquainted with

Mr. An, but from the way he talked and his mannerisms, my husband and I received the impression that he was a forthright young man. Here was testimony that corroborated what Mr. Ishidaka had heard, and from a totally separate source. For my husband and myself, it was enough to convince us that Megumi was indeed in North Korea.

Two days later, on February 8, Asahi National Broadcasting aired Mr. An's testimony as part of Mr. Takase's report on its program, *The Scoop.* On this program, however, neither Mr. An's name nor face appeared on the screen.

Then, on March 13, the *Sankei Shimbun*'s morning edition devoted a large section to a series of questions and answers between journalist Akihiko Ota and Mr. An. This time, Mr. An's name appeared in the article, along with a picture of him, his head bowed, looking at Megumi's picture.

I would like to extract part of the questions and answers from the *Sankei Shimbun*, although some portions overlap with the passage from Mr. Takase's book:

Ota: I hear that you saw a Japanese woman [when you were still in North Korea].

An: On October 10, 1988, there was a ceremony to commemorate the founding of the Workers' Party at the Political and Military University on the outskirts of Pyongyang. I graduated from this university in the 25th graduating class, but at that time I was still in my second year. I saw a woman who looked Japanese at a gathering marking the ceremony. One of the instructors, a man named Chon, who was a graduate of the 11th class or possibly earlier, spotted her and said, "I brought her here from Niigata." That was when I found out that she had been abducted from Japan.

Ota: When was she abducted?

An: I don't remember the exact date, but Instructor Chon said that it was in the early to mid seventies. He said that three spies took part in the abduction. Two of them were headed towards the sea, walking near the coast, when she came by. They feared that she would report seeing them, so they abducted her. I've heard that she was not wearing the clothes she is wearing in the picture. [The school uniform. Mr. An was shown the photo used in the investigation.] After she was put on the ship, and throughout the voyage, she never stopped crying. That was when they realized they had abducted a child.

Ota: What happened to her after she arrived in North Korea?

An: She wouldn't stop crying. She didn't eat, either. The men were chastised for abducting a mere child. The girl was told, "You should study Korean. If you study, you will be taken

back to Japan; we can give you a job as well."
She mastered Korean but since she wasn't
allowed to return to Japan, she became ill. I
have heard that she was hospitalized twice
at Hospital 915, near the university.

Ota: How did she seem when you saw her?

An: She was sitting about twenty to thirty
meters away from me, wearing a navy suit
and a white blouse. She was with two or
three other women, and she was talking
and laughing like any woman might.
From the way she laughed, I got the impression that she was pretty outgoing. She
seemed to be about twenty-five or twenty-
six years old, and she may have been
wearing high-heeled shoes. She was about
160 centimeters tall and appeared to be
unmarried. She had a round, full face and
wore her hair straight with bangs cut across
her forehead. She wore a little more make-
up than other women in North Korea, and
seemed somehow different from them. I
saw her again around January 1989, and
I wondered then if she had really been
abducted. Instructor Chon said that he had
seen her a few times and had tried to talk
to her, but she ignored him each time. No
doubt she disliked him.

Ota: What was her life like?

An: She lived near the university and I doubt that

she was allowed to go out much. However, she was a valuable instructor of Japanese, so by North Korean standards she lived comfortably. I doubt that she suffered from poverty. I lost interest after that period, so I don't know what has happened to her since.

Mr. Takase's book mentions also that Megumi looked well, and Mr. An recalls, "She seemed to be good friends with another Japanese woman. I have seen her walking hand in hand with the woman, and the two of them were laughing together." At least Megumi looked well when Mr. An saw her, but there is no way of knowing what she faced after she was taken to North Korea. Poor Megumi had cried throughout the voyage, couldn't eat, and was hospitalized twice. How frightened and lonely she must have been. I read the article feeling as though someone were ripping my heart out.

To Seoul

When I read the testimony that the spies were headed toward the sea when they passed a girl and abducted her, my memory was jolted.

Twenty years earlier, on the day Megumi disappeared, two suspicious-looking men had followed a high school girl who lived near us. This happened about 30 minutes before Megumi and her friend had parted to

go their separate ways. The young girl had graduated
Yorii Middle School a few years ahead of Megumi, and
her brother was in the same grade as our daughter.

At about six o'clock that day, the young girl was
walking home on the street that leads to the sea, when
she saw two men walking towards her from the direction
of the beach. The young girl said that chills ran down
her spine when they passed, for she saw up close their
menacing, hard-featured faces, tanned the color of
copper. When she looked back after a few steps, she was
alarmed to discover that they were right behind her.
They had turned around and begun following her.

She said that she was ready to take a swing with
the tennis racket in her hand, but they stopped following her. When she turned to look back again a little
further on, she saw that they were talking, looking in
her direction. She ran all the way to her house as fast as
she could and leaped inside. "Mother, it was terrifying!"
she cried. The mother opened the window and looked
out, but didn't see anyone. The young girl also saw a
car parked in an empty lot near the entrance to the site
of the former science building. The young girl told the
police her story as soon as she heard about Megumi.

Another woman also witnessed a suspicious
looking car that same day. The woman was the mother
of a friend of Megumi's. She worked as a volunteer at
a nearby facility for mentally handicapped children.
She saw a light-colored car on her way home from the
facility. As she walked by, the window suddenly opened,
and an arm shot out and waved to her as if beckoning

her to come. She, too, became frightened and ran as fast as she could away from the car.

On another occasion, shortly after we learned that Megumi was in North Korea, my husband and I were contacting Megumi's friends when we learned that a student in the badminton club had seen a white car parked on the street that day, on the north side of the school grounds. Since a large hospital fronted the street, private vehicles were normally prohibited from parking on that stretch of road.

When I put everything together, I can't help but think that Megumi was abducted, not because she had witnessed North Korean spies, but because the spies had planned to kidnap any woman who was walking along a dark street alone. The street she was walking would have been so dark that even if Megumi had seen them, she would have just walked by and not noticed anything, for it is doubtful that they were carrying anything that would immediately identify them as spies.

But I have digressed.

Prior to the publication on March 13 of the interview between Mr. Ota and Mr. An in *Sankei Shimbun*, my husband and I were invited by Mr. Ishidaka to accompany him and his crew to South Korea and meet Mr. An.

We left for South Korea on March 14 and met Mr. An the next day. We talked for three to four hours, but because everything had to be translated, I think the actual conversation was about two hours long. My husband and I were impressed with Mr. An's courteous attitude and manner of speaking. After we met him, we knew that what Mr. An said was not to be doubted.

I was very nervous before the meeting; the fact that he was a former spy conjured a menacing figure in my mind. Mr. Ishidaka had gone to meet him at the front entrance, but it was some time before Mr. An came to the room where we were waiting. I wondered why he did not come, and thought that perhaps he had changed his mind about meeting us.

I later heard that Mr. An had indeed felt hesitant. While he was not directly involved with Megumi's abduction, he felt guilty about meeting her parents because of his former association with the people who had carried out the deed. Also, Mr. Ishidaka had not told him much about us when he had requested the meeting.

About ten or fifteen minutes after the appointed time, a dashing young man wearing a suit and tie came into the room. *He looks like a normal young man,* I thought with relief. My husband and I stood up and introduced ourselves. "We are glad to meet you. We are Megumi's parents." He returned our greeting rather nervously.

We talked about a lot of things, most of which have been covered in the *Sankei Shimbun* article. What we heard for the first time that day was that Mr. An's instructor, Chon, had infiltrated Japan a number of times after kidnapping Megumi. On one of those occasions, he spotted a flyer with Megumi's picture that had been circulated during the investigation. He had taken it down and brought it back to North Korea as a souvenir and kept it since.

We had a copy of the flyer with the picture of Megumi wearing her school uniform. We showed our copy and asked him if this was what he had seen. Unfortunately, Mr. An had only heard about what Chon had done, and never had the opportunity to see the flyer itself.

At the end of our meeting, we showed Mr. An a picture of Megumi taken a month before her disappearance, when we went to Niigata Airport to see her grandfather off. Seeing this photo, he said with conviction, "This picture most strongly resembles the woman I saw."

Seeing Mr. An sitting across from me, the thought crossed my mind that he was also a victim of the regime, forced to live a life not of his choosing. "You are all victims as well," I said with sympathy. Mr. An replied, "I also have parents, brothers, and sisters. I had to leave them behind. Megumi is there as well, while her parents are here. I can tell how truly concerned you are about her. In the same way, I am concerned about my parents."

I could only reply, "I have always prayed for Megumi's safety. From now on, I'll include your parents in my prayers as well." Hearing my words, Mr. An appeared visibly moved.

Throughout our meeting, personnel from the Agency for National Security Planning stood in the back, discreetly listening to our conversation. The NSP staffers later told Mr. Ishidaka that after Mr. An left us, he burst into tears. It surprised them, as they had never seen him cry like that before.

It could not have been easy for Mr. An to meet us. For mothers and fathers, a child will always remain in their hearts no matter what happens, and children feel the same love for their parents. I think this is universal, irrespective of nationality. After meeting Mr. An, whenever I pray for Megumi and ask that she be kept out of harm's way, I always ask the same for Mr. An's parents, brothers, and sisters.

Two days after our meeting with Mr. An, on the 17th, we visited Panmunjom.* Along the way, there were a number of gates or arches made of heavy concrete. I was told that if North Korea ever invaded South Korea, these gates would be blown up with explosives to stop the advancement of North Korean tanks. As we neared Panmunjom, I saw bridges that were so narrow that only one vehicle could cross at a time. It was a chilling reminder that the possibility of war was never far off.

The date of our visit happened to be the day before Hwang Jang-Yop, the North Korean Secretary-General who had sought political asylum in China, was scheduled to leave China. There were rumors that he would be flown immediately to South Korea, so tanks and armed soldiers were everywhere. The tight security made me nervous. The message was all too clear that

---

* Panmunjom lies just south of the 38th parallel, the military demar-cation line that separates North and South Korea.

the war had not ended, that the present conditions constituted only a ceasefire.

From Panmunjom, I could see the bare mountains of North Korea. Soldiers from North and South faced each other over the border. We were prohibited from addressing the North's troops, but seeing them standing there in their khaki uniforms, without any expression on their faces, and thinking of Megumi living amongst them, it was all I could do to stop myself from shouting at them, "Give me back my Megumi!"

Does Megumi Have Dimples?

After our return to Japan, my husband and I formed the Association of the Families of Victims Kidnapped by North Korea. Later in this book, I would like to explain how this association came into existence and our activities, such as petitions to the government.

After the broadcast of his first testimony, Mr. An received many requests from the Japanese media for interviews. Mr. An testified to the abductions, and allowed his name and pictures of his face to appear in print and on television. The more I learned about North Korea, the more I realized that this was truly a courageous act.

Then suddenly, on October 30, 1997, about six months after our meeting with Mr. An, the newspaper *Sankei Shimbun* published an article that read:

An official of the Foreign Ministry who oversees the North Korean situation expressed grave doubts regarding the reliability of testimony by a former North Korean spy with regard to the alleged abductions of Japanese by North Korean agents. The official stated on the afternoon of the 29th that since this testimony is a key piece of evidence supporting the suspicion of abduction by North Korea, Japan should, in his view, proceed with caution in its response.

According to the paper, this Foreign Ministry official stated that "spies will say anything." When my husband was asked for his reaction to this statement, he replied that he was outraged.

Within the same day, the official's statement was amended and *Sankei Shimbun* duly noted this. Needless to say, the statement angered not only my husband, but also Mr. An, who heard the news in Korea. He decided to write a book recounting his experiences so that people would realize that he had testified to the truth despite the grave risk to his life. His book, *North Korean Abduction Operative*, was translated into Japanese and published by Tokuma Shoten in March 1998.

About a month before the book's publication, Mr. Takase called. "This may sound like a strange question," he said, "but does Megumi have dimples?" The question took me completely by surprise and I needed a moment to think.

Yes, she did have a dimple, but it wasn't conspicuous. I asked Mr. Takase to hold so that I could look at her pictures to make sure. After looking in an album, I found two pictures of her smiling and sure enough, there were dimples. Because she has a round face and the dimples were inconspicuous, they appeared only with a broad smile.

Mr. Takase explained the reason for his question. He had been asked to read the draft of the book Mr. An was writing in response to the Foreign Ministry official's statement. Reading the advance copy, Mr. Takase's attention was riveted to a description of the woman that Mr. An had said resembled Megumi. Mr. An had written, "When she smiled, her dimples gave the impression that she had a sweet disposition." If Megumi did not have dimples, the woman Mr. An had seen could not be Megumi, and it would be a case of mistaken identity. Mr. Takase had become concerned, and had phoned us to confirm whether Megumi had a dimple or not.

We had never mentioned Megumi's dimples to the police, so it wasn't in the flyer we had distributed. It is rather embarrassing as a mother to admit this, but I had forgotten about her dimples. My husband, on the other hand, had not thought that dimples were a particularly distinctive facial feature since he and all of his siblings had dimples.

It is doubtful that Mr. An could fabricate a story based on a feature that we, Megumi's own parents, had overlooked. And meeting Mr. An had convinced us of the veracity of what he had to say. After Megumi's dimples came to light, our belief became a deep conviction and we decided to never lose hope that Megumi was indeed alive in North Korea.

We later read Mr. An's book, *North Korean Abduction Operative*, and found a particularly wrenching description of Megumi's abduction:

> According to the instructor who took part in Megumi's abduction, Megumi cried so wildly on board the ship that they confined her to a pitch-dark storage room for over forty hours. Incarcerated in the storage room, Megumi continued to cry for her mother, and clawed the doorway and walls with her bare hands. When they arrived in North Korea, they saw that the girl's hands were bloody and raw, her nails almost torn off...

When I read this, I felt sick to my stomach. But tears did not come this time. At that moment, I felt not sadness, but a deep, deep anger welling up inside me.

Chapter V
IF I COULD TAKE HER PLACE

Dreams of My Daughter

After my daughter went missing, I had five dreams over the course of two years. Even now, I remember these five dreams vividly. In my first dream, Megumi and I were standing on the wooden deck of a pier, waiting for a ferry. We could not yet see the ferry, but we were waiting to board it. The river in front of us was not very wide, and there was a greenish cast to the water. There were many people in line behind us. My daughter looked very pale beside me. Her raincoat was the color of celadon; it was not the raincoat that she habitually wore. I was engulfed by an overwhelming sense of loneliness and felt very uneasy. It was an indescribably unpleasant dream and I was jolted awake.

In my next dream, I saw the shoe rack at the entry of the school.* I was standing by the shoe rack and one of the detectives who had taken part in the search for my daughter approached me and said, "Mrs. Yokota, this is indeed terrible. It is so cold-blooded that I have no words to speak."

I saw a black plastic bag that had been left in the corner. One hears of homicides in which the victim's body is dismembered and disposed of in a plastic bag. From the detective's words, I instinctively understood that something similar had happened.

It felt as though the blood had frozen in my veins. Filled with terror, I bolted awake.

My next dream also had images of water. It was a dream in which I rescued a kitten that was drowning in the ocean.

As I was walking along the shore with my deceased mother, I saw that a tiny kitten was drowning. I love cats and, wanting to help it, I waded into the ocean. I could not swim, but the water became deeper and deeper. I came to the point where I would drown if I went any further. My mother, wearing a kimono, was right behind me, saying, "Be careful, be careful."

I stretched out my arm as far as I could and was able to catch the kitten. I said to the kitten, "I'm so glad you are all right," and clasped it to my heart. My

---

* In Japan, shoe racks are placed by the entrance of the school. Students remove the shoes they wear to school, place them in the racks, and change to a pair kept for school.

Five months old, with her father in Nagoya

Her first birthday

Almost a year old, 1965

Three years old, at the zoo

A very spirited girl

"You ate a lot of spaghetti!"

With her brothers Takuya (r) and Tetsuya

She liked to take care of her brothers

Celebrating Children's Day

Megumi (1) enters kindergarten, 1969

With her pet Java sparrow

With her brothers at a Hiroshima zoo; they were all fond of animals

First time skating; an athletic girl, she quickly got the hang of it

Fashionable even on the rink

Family portrait, Hiroshima, 1972

She often made faces for the camera...

...since she loved to make people laugh

She liked to walk: hiking in 1973

Fourth grade: a dimpled smile on Sports Day

L to r: Tetsuya, friend Ako, Megumi, and Takuya

Megumi (r) at a zoo with a friend

Fifth grade: getting set to run-walk

Family trip; Megumi's clothes handmade by her mother

At a park the family visited often on Sundays

Serious ballerina, standing on her toes

On a trip with her mother, 1974

Gathering seashells, 1975

Megumi on sixth-grade school trip

In Kyoto, her mother's hometown

She had really looked forward to this trip

First winter in snow country; she often said, "This place is cold"

At the zoo on a company trip, courtesy of the BOJ

Sado Island: last trip before her abduction

Niigata, 1976: after a fireworks festival

Seeing off her grandfather (last photo prior to her abduction)

Megumi was kidnapped not far from this beach one year later

Association of the Families of Victims Kidnapped by North Korea, March 26, 1997 press conference in Tokyo (© The Asahi Shimbun)

Her father pleads for the case's swift resolution (© The Asahi Shimbun)

Calling for signatures in the streets of Niigata, May 5, 1997

Oil painting of Megumi by her mother

A photograph considered to be of Megumi, approx. 20 yrs old; provided by North Korea to a Japanese fact-finding delegation in 2002

Woman claimed to be Megumi, in a photo marked "1986.8.3" and released in 2006 by Kim Yong-nam, also pictured

Also released by Kim, family portrait with baby Hye-gyong

Kim Hye-gyong in Pyongyang in 2002, holding photo of grandparents (© The Asahi Shimbun)

October 15, 2002: Five abductees visit Japan after 24-year absence (© The Asahi Shimbun)

Kim Hye-gyong, age 15; portraits on the wall are of Kim Il-sung and Kim Jong-il (© The Asahi Shimbun)

mother said also, "Yes, I am so glad," and looked very happy. This was my third dream. Megumi did not appear in this dream, but I remember it very distinctly because it was one of the strange dreams that I had around that period.

In my fourth dream, I was sitting in a noodle shop with my mother sitting across from me. A young girl came up to our table to take our order, saying, "What would you like?" I looked at her face and was surprised. It was Megumi. I said, "Oh, Megumi! Why are you here? We were so worried about you. But I'm so glad. You are all right and you were right here. " At my words, Megumi's face lit up and she smiled.

My fifth dream was also a strange one. I was standing in front of an apartment building that looked about five floors high and was still under construction. Not a window or anything was in place, so it looked like a large concrete shell. Looking up, I could see light shining on a floor that was high up in the building. And Megumi, who looked about two and a half or three years old, was happily running around by herself on the floor. *Why is she running around by herself in such a dangerous place?* I thought.

My husband says that he sometimes dreams of Megumi as a child going to elementary school, playing with her younger brothers. However, after that dream set in the apartment building, I can hardly recall having any other dreams about her. This is why my five dreams are so vivid and unforgettable. I remember very clearly the color of the river, the color of the ocean, and the color of the raincoat my daughter was wearing...

Did my daughter run away from home? Could she have committed suicide? Had she been involved in an accident? Not knowing whether she was alive or dead, but believing that she must surely be alive somewhere, I somehow managed to live on without my daughter. Then suddenly, in 1997, twenty years after her disappearance, I received surprising news. A former spy who had defected to South Korea from the North had testified that he had seen Megumi in Pyongyang. I also heard that several other spies had separately given similar testimony.

So I discovered that my daughter, who had seemingly vanished, had actually been spirited away to North Korea. I also learned that there were many other Japanese in North Korea who, like Megumi, had been abducted. Many of them were young—in their twenties—at the time of their disappearance, and were kidnapped at about the same time Megumi was. Their parents have no doubt spent the ensuing years in the same kind of unbearable despair as we have. Many of them are now old and I have heard that some are bedridden.

While I felt immense relief that my daughter may still be alive, I also felt faint thinking how difficult it would be to rescue my daughter and others from an insular country like North Korea.

These young people were abducted without any reason, robbed of the flower of their youth to become prisoners in a world of darkness. When I think of these homesick children, longing for their homes but not daring even to breathe their hopes under the merciless watch of their captors, and when I think of their twenty long years under such conditions, I feel as though my heart is being ripped out. I am filled with desperate urgency—if I could take their place, I would fly to them right now. I believe that any parent would understand this feeling.

Recently, for the first time in twenty years, I had another vivid dream of my daughter. I don't know where I was in this dream, but my daughter appeared in my dream like magic. By now, my daughter would be 34 years old, but in my dream she was of high school age and hadn't changed much from the last time I had seen her. I said to her, "Oh, you look well. I am so glad!" My daughter smiled as if to say, "Yes, I'm glad too." She had the same old carefree smile, and it seemed as if nothing had happened.

If only this dream could become a reality. I cannot help but pray that all those abducted children may return safely back to Japan while their elderly parents are still able to welcome them home.

A New Challenge

After Megumi's disappearance, I started painting, though I have never received formal instruction. My first painting was an oil portrait of Megumi that I painted while looking at a picture of her. In the photo, taken when she was small, she has long hair to her shoulders, which she wore in two plaits adorned with ribbons. Since I knew nothing of how to use a brush or mix colors, it is not really a painting that I can show to other people. Still, the painting is dear to me because the memory of Megumi, with her plaited hair swaying gently while busy at play, is very sweet. Even though it was just a painting, I wanted to feel that Megumi was near me.

I also started to write *tanka* poems, into which I wove memories of my daughter. My first *tanka* poem was this sad one:

Together from far away we moved
To this land of snow where
Oceans wail for my daughter lost

The ritual of turning off the porch light every morning, which I always made sure was kept on all night while we lived in Niigata. Or discovering a tiny flower blooming on the cactus plant that Megumi brought home from a school trip. Walking along the road that leads to Yorii Middle School. These were the source of my *tanka* poems.

Early every morning
The birds sing in sadness
The pale porch light beams
Waiting for three years

My child vanishes
Leaving a cactus plant
A small blossom comes to life
And so my daughter too, I hope

My tears like dewdrops
I water the flower
Left by my lost daughter
For me to watch over

Under the autumn sky
The road stretches to the pale beyond
Secrets kept, never revealed
Vanishing to the unknown

About the time when Megumi would have graduated middle school, I often went for solitary walks along the beach. One day, I saw girls who might have been Megumi's age playing along the shore.

If these events hadn't happened, Megumi might have been among them, lost in carefree play. Here is the poem I composed:

Ready to leave the nest
Young girls frolic and play
I call my daughter's name
She who is gone and has yet to return

On another occasion, I stared for a long time at a red buoy floating in the sea, because it looked like the red bag that my daughter had carried on that fateful day. This tanka came to me then:

Sado and the ocean beyond, stained crimson
I stare and stand at the shore
Feeling my soul
Touched by God

The crimson color of the sunset held me rapt, and I could feel my soul being pulled into it and swept out to an infinite horizon beyond.

I walked along long stretches of the shore weeping for my daughter, looking for anything that might have belonged to her. I knew that she had been snatched away from somewhere along that shoreline. Could such a reprehensible act ever be forgiven? The mere idea of abducting a girl and taking her across the sea is so barbaric that it feels as though it could happen only in a story. But this was the frightening reality.

The call we received from Mr. Hyomoto on January 21, 1997, asking my husband to come to the Diet Members' Building, changed the tide of our life. Since then, my husband and I have tried frantically to keep up with each new development. In the beginning, I was filled with a feeling of joy so powerful that I almost shivered: my daughter was alive.

But even as I felt this surge, my heart sank as I considered the reality of conditions in North Korea. These somber feelings merged with all the other emotions that I had carried with me since November 15, 1977, when Megumi disappeared. My recollections of those days are like a nightmare in which one is skinned alive. I recall the air—so dense and cold that I want to scream in fear.

Now, the nightmare had begun again, and my emotions were in turmoil. This time, however, with the words of the Bible as my support, I vowed to accept the changed circumstances as a new challenge in my life. Recovering from my early confusion and panic, I was able to regain some peace within myself.

Despite this renewed resolve, there was still frustration. Because her disappearance had become a matter to be resolved between two nations, I could not think of a single thing I could do to regain my daughter, or even confirm her safety for that matter. It felt as though it was all beyond the reach of a single individual.

For a long time, I had been an ordinary housewife. I had worked for a while after graduating high school, but the idea of a woman working after marriage was a novel one at the time. After my marriage, I devoted myself to my children and our home, and my link to the world outside was limited to occasional stints as a volunteer. It had never occurred to me that the relationship between Japan and North Korea would be of such immediate concern to me.

Since Megumi's disappearance, all my thoughts and prayers were for her safety, that somehow, somewhere, she was alive. Now, from this personal level, the issue had ballooned to international proportions. I knew what I was up against; the wall in front of me seemed impenetrable, and my power as an individual seemed impossibly small. I felt so powerless that I couldn't sleep at night.

But, to my infinite gratitude, there were people, strangers to me, who were concerned about the abductions. With their concerted efforts, steps were being taken to rescue Megumi.

The First Petition

On February 7, 1997, Representative Nishimura held a press conference after receiving the government's response to his inquiry. My husband and I attended the conference to express our opinions from the parents' perspective. That evening, we left for Niigata with Mr. Kenji Ishidaka of Asahi Broadcasting, who was going to conduct research. During this visit, we had the opportunity to meet Harunori Kojima.

Mr. Kojima was an acquaintance of Katsumi Sato, the Director of the Modern Korea Institute. Mr. Kojima had written a letter to us upon our return from Niigata a week earlier, and for the first time we became aware of his activities.

In the mid-1950s there was a movement to help Koreans living in Japan to return to their homeland, North Korea. In those days, newspapers were depicting North Korea as a "heaven on earth," so a large number of Koreans returned there with dreams of a better life. Among these people were Japanese women who had married Korean men. They are now referred to in the Japanese media simply as the "wives from Japan."

Mr. Kojima and Mr. Sato had become acquainted because they were both working for the Japanese agency that helped repatriate these people to North Korea. Later, they learned that North Korea was far from being a "heaven on earth," and that the people who had been repatriated were suffering great hardship. Both Mr. Sato and Mr. Kojima felt responsible for helping to send so many people back to North Korea, so Mr. Kojima started a movement to help these people, the "wives from Japan" in particular, to return to Japan.

Those who had relocated to North Korea sent letters to their families in Japan depicting the misery of their lives. Mr. Kojima helped make sure that the letters reached their destinations, and compiled the letters into a booklet that he published and distributed.

Mr. Kojima lived in Niigata and had read Mr. Ishidaka's article in the October 1996 *Modern Korea*. At the time, he did not make the connection between the abducted girl in the article and Megumi. But in December he attended Mr. Sato's lecture in Niigata City and the reception that followed. It was on this occasion that a member of the police force attending the lecture recognized the abducted girl as Megumi. Mr. Kojima recalled the case and went to the library to reread the piece that had appeared in the *Niigata Nippo*.

Late that year, when Mr. Kojima and his associates were having an end-of-the-year party, they discussed how their cause and our quest for Megumi had a great deal in common. Since we both had to deal with North Korea, they thought that it made sense to combine our efforts. They also thought that, because Megumi had been abducted in Niigata, it was fitting that the people of Niigata should try to rescue her.

Mr. Kojima came to us and suggested that we collect signatures together to petition the government to investigate the abductions and rescue those who were kidnapped, as well as to petition jointly for the support of various government agencies. Soon, he and his associates had formed the Citizens for Inquiry and the Rescue of Megumi Yokota.

As Mr. Kojima relayed to me what he was trying to accomplish, it occurred to me that I was hearing of a situation that I never knew existed. It was especially disturbing that the Japanese women who had accompanied their husbands to North Korea had no way of coming back to Japan for visits. Even those who had crossed to North Korea of their own free will could not come back. I worried whether Megumi, who had been taken there against her will, had any chance of ever coming home.

The thought that Megumi was in such a country made me anxious, but even so, I felt fortunate to have met people who were familiar with the situation there. These people had offered their help and I felt encouraged.

On February 14, we accompanied Mr. Kojima and his associates to make the rounds of the Foreign Ministry, the Diet and the Japanese Red Cross to ask for assistance in the repatriation effort.

It was my first visit to the Kasumigaseki district where the ministerial offices are located, and to Nagata-cho, where the Diet and the Prime Minister's official residence are. I had never thought that I would find myself in this part of Tokyo. There was a distinctive feel to the area, and I became very nervous. It was all I could do to accompany my husband and Mr. Kojima, so I hardly had the presence of mind to be aware of my surroundings.

At the Foreign Ministry, Ryozo Kato, Director General of the Asian Affairs Bureau at the time, greeted us at the doorway of his room. He promised us that the government would do everything possible to help with repatriation.

Mr. Kato later called to update us on the progress. His first call came on June 10 and the second on July 30, immediately after his return from the ASEAN Ministerial Meeting, to which he had accompanied then Foreign Minister Yukihiko Ikeda.

During his second call, he told my husband, "At this time, the temporary return of the 'wives from

Japan' has received all the attention in the media. I am sure that this is of some concern for the families of those who were abducted. I want to assure you that the government continues to view the abductions and illegal drug trade as major issues to be negotiated with the North Korean government. My regret is that we have little to report to the families, since we have made no progress." Since then, my husband and I have put our faith in Mr. Kato, and have placed our hopes on the negotiations by the Foreign Ministry.

On our February 14 visit, most of the people we visited at the Diet Members' Building were representatives from Niigata. Each representative listened earnestly to what we had to say, and I felt encouraged. On April 1, a number of representatives formed a group called the Liberal Democratic Party Diet Members of Niigata. We petitioned the group to obtain information from the Foreign Ministry and the National Police Agency, and to negotiate for the return of Japanese citizens with firmness and resolve. As a result of our appeal, more representatives joined on April 15 to form a nonpartisan group, The Association of Representatives to Rescue Japanese Nationals Abducted by North Korea.

At our next destination, the Japanese Red Cross, the Planning Section of the International Department asked us to submit a "Document of Inquiry." It was explained to us that there was little the Red Cross could do without the cooperation of the country in question. The Red Cross would send this document to their counterparts in North Korea, but we could only wait for the reply.

The manner in which the steps were explained to us was very smooth and polite, but somehow impersonal. I was nervous because I had never taken part in such discussions before; even so, the person's manner struck me as indifferent. It sounded as though he were parroting something memorized from a manual. This made me realize the difficulty of our mission without the benefit of an influential supporter for our cause.

My husband and I visited the Red Cross again the following week to submit the "Document of Inquiry." To this day, we have heard nothing.

That summer, the North Korean government agreed to investigate the people on the list of "Possible Victims of Abduction" submitted by Japan as "Miscellaneous Missing Persons." But on June 5, 1998, the following year, the government announced through a spokesman for the North Korean Red Cross Central Committee that, "As a result of our investigation, we are satisfied that it has been proven that the ten people on the list have never lived in North Korea. Nor is there any record of their having entered or temporarily resided in North Korea at any time."

Since this was the official government position, it was impossible of course to get a reply that said otherwise to a "Document of Inquiry" submitted by an individual.

Since our first round of petitions with Mr. Kojima on February 14, 1997, we have pleaded our cause in front of countless people. I remember most of the places we have visited, but not all. My husband, however, kept a record that shows that, in two years alone, we visited—among others—Amnesty International, the Civil Liberties Bureau of the Ministry of Justice, the Japan Federation of Bar Associations, and the Civil Liberties Committee. Individually, we appealed to Representative Masaaki Nakayama, the leader of the Liberal Democratic Party's North Korean Mission at the time; then-Foreign Minister Keizo Obuchi; Keizo Takemi, Vice Minister of the Foreign Ministry; Ichiro Ozawa, leader of the Liberal Democratic Party; Mr. Obuchi again, after he became Prime Minister; Foreign Minister Masahiko Koumura; and many, many others.

No matter how many times I take part in a petition, it does not get easier for me. My husband is able to talk calmly, and I am full of admiration for his composure. I become emotional and I always regret it later.

In particular, I recall a visit to the Civil Liberties Bureau of the Ministry of Justice as one of my worst moments, for it was an infuriating experience. Even now, I can't recall the occasion without feeling angry.

Our visit took place on October 6, 1998. The bureau staff member who received us agreed that abduction is "an extreme violation of the individual's human rights." And yet, according to this person, the main responsibility of the Civil Liberties Bureau was to arbitrate matters such as noise pollution claims among apartment dwellers, and to oversee such human rights problems as the protection of privacy versus the rights of the media.

It seemed to me that many of his comments contradicted what one would expect from the name "Civil Liberties Bureau." My husband made a note of what we heard: according to this official, "there is no precedent in which a claim was made for human rights violations of a Japanese citizen residing outside of Japan," and that in our case, it was "more of a criminal issue than a human rights issue." Of course, "repatriation [of the victim] would solve the human rights issue, but the negotiations for his or her return would be the Foreign Ministry's responsibility." We were also told that, "As civil servants, members of the Foreign Ministry naturally have an obligation to protect individual rights. However, the Justice Ministry is not empowered to make any recommendations to the Foreign Ministry."

When my husband inquired, "If you think it is a criminal case, should we go to the Criminal Affairs Bureau?" this official replied, "I don't know if the Criminal Affairs Bureau can handle a case such as this. In any case, I shall make a report to my superior. My superior will decide what we can do about it."

I sat listening to words that sounded as though they had come out of a textbook, and I began to feel angry. Normally, when I accompanied my husband to make an appeal, I said very little, except to say greetings and introduce myself. But this time, I couldn't help speaking. "You tell me that these are the rules and some department or bureau or other will handle it. But this is such a grave matter that everyone needs to sit down together to find a solution."

The bureau employee sat and listened with a sour expression. I wondered later if I had been too outspoken, but since this was the bureau that was supposed to protect civil liberties, I had hoped that they would offer constructive advice. My disappointment was all the greater because of my feeling of betrayal.

The people at the Japan Federation of Bar Associations and Amnesty International listened intently to what we had to say, but I learned that there was a limit to what they could do. It was possible for the Federation to submit a recommendation to the government with regard to the abduction, and activities could be pursued to raise the issue of human rights at the United Nations and build public awareness. However, recommendations made by the United Nations are non-binding, so North Korea could choose to ignore them without fear of repercussions.

As it became apparent how complex the reality was, I would sometimes become discouraged. Each time, however, I would recall in my mind Megumi's face and tell myself that I couldn't give up.

My husband feels that although we do not see tangible progress, the government and Foreign Ministry are proceeding with negotiations. He tells me that, due to the political or diplomatic nature of the negotiations, there are things that cannot be disclosed to the families of those abducted.

I understand what my husband is saying, of course. Still, as a mother, I cannot help but wish that our representatives would raise the abduction issue at the negotiating table, even at the risk of complicating Japan's talks with North Korea. Those entrusted with the negotiations have an obligation to produce real results, and be fearless in acting to ensure the safety of their countrymen.

The Tragedy of the Families Left Behind

Soon after we met Mr. Hyomoto, Councilor Hashimoto's secretary and the man who had called my husband, it became clear to us that he had been doing research on the abductions for a considerable time. He later told us that he learned of the abductions while he was following the case of the Korean Airlines flight that was blown up in November 1987.

The man and woman responsible for this bombing were spies from North Korea posing as a Japanese couple. When the two were arrested, they immediately tried to commit suicide by taking cyanide pills. The male suspect died, but the woman miraculously survived. Her name was Kim Hyon Hui. Kim testified that when she was trained as a spy, a Japanese woman named "Li Un Hae" had taught her Japanese. From this woman, Kim had also been instructed in the details of daily living, learning all she would need to live like an ordinary Japanese woman. If this Li Un Hae were Japanese, it was possible she was one of the women abducted in 1978, when a number of couples disappeared. Upon further investigation, Japanese police identified "Li" as Yaeko Taguchi, who has been missing since 1978.

It was at this point that Mr. Hyomoto learned of the disappearance of three couples. In 1988, he personally visited the families of those who had disappeared, specifically, those of Kaoru Hasuike of Niigata and Yasushi Chimura and Fukie Hamamoto of Fukui. He also traveled to Kagoshima to learn more about the disappearance of Shuichi Ichikawa and Rumiko Masumoto.

Each of the families in turn told Mr. Hyomoto that their loved ones had disappeared without a trace: there were no indications that they had met with an accident, nor was there any suspicion that they had planned to run away. In fact, each person had vanished as if he or she had been swept off the face of the earth. Councilor Hashimoto's questions at the Upper House Budget Committee in 1988 were based on facts researched by Mr. Hyomoto on these trips.

Despite the statement by Seiroku Kajiyama, Chairman of the National Public Safety Commission, that the government recognized "the strong possibility that the abductions were ordered by North Korea," seven years passed without any further developments. Then, in 1995, Kenji Ishidaka of Asahi Broadcasting heard from An Myon Jin that he may have seen one of the men, Shuichi Ichikawa, in North Korea. When word of this new revelation reached Mr. Hyomoto, he visited the six families of the three abducted couples again and convinced them to form an association of victims, in order to bring public attention to bear on what had taken place. Shortly before the mass media reports that Megumi had been seen in North Korea, these families had decided to form such an association.

Thus on March 25, a month after numerous publications reported the discovery that Megumi had been abducted to North Korea, the Association of the Families of Victims Kidnapped by North Korea was established, thanks to the combined efforts of Mr. Hyomoto and Mr. Ishidaka. Mr. Hyomoto had contacted us to suggest that my husband and I also join.

The members that gathered that day were the Chimura and Hamamoto families of Fukui, the Hasuike family of Niigata, the Ichikawa and Masumoto families of Kagoshima, the Arimoto family of Kobe, and my husband and myself. At the meeting, my husband was chosen to represent the association. The family of Tadaaki Hara from Nagasaki also became members, but were unable to attend the first meeting. Since the first meeting, Yukiko Okudo's family has joined as well, so we are now nine families strong.

Other than Ms. Arimoto, the other victims were all included in the government's official list of "six incidents, total of nine victims" thought to be abducted by North Korea. Although I had become familiar with the disappearance of the three couples through the newspapers, I learned of Mr. Hara and Ms. Arimoto on the day of our first meeting.

Mr. Hara was 49 years old when he was abducted in 1980. He had been a cook at a Chinese restaurant in Osaka and was abducted because a North Korean spy wanted to use his identity. Mr. Hara had become a target since he and the spy were near each other in age, and because Mr. Hara did not have close family who might search for him. The spy was caught five years later in South Korea and charged with espionage. Because he was using Mr. Hara's identity, the latter's disappearance came to light.

Keiko Arimoto was 23 years old when she disappeared. She was studying in England and vanished in July 1983 while visiting Copenhagen. She had told her parents that she would return to Japan on August 9 and had even informed them of the flight number. Her parents had done everything possible to trace her whereabouts, but without success.

Five years after Ms. Arimoto's disappearance, in 1988, her family received surprising news from a family in Sapporo. A man who was originally from Hokkaido had written to his family there that he, Ms. Arimoto, and another young man from Kumamoto were all in Pyongyang, and that he wished his family to contact the families of Ms. Arimoto and the young man from Kumamoto. The second young man had been a graduate student at the Kyoto University of Foreign Languages. When the Arimotos pursued this matter, they found out that the young men from Sapporo and Kumamoto had both been studying abroad when they disappeared in 1980. They were last seen in Spain.

Later, the families were to see a picture taken by a man who had become acquainted in Europe with the young man from Sapporo. His picture shows the young man at a zoo in Barcelona, sitting on a bench with two women, all smiling. What makes this picture ominous is that the two women are the wives of the Japanese Red Army members who hijacked the Japan Air Lines flight to North Korea in 1970 (the "Yodo Incident").

It was all very mysterious. What was apparent, however, was that the North Koreans abducted not only Japanese people from Japan, but also Japanese living in Europe.

Although the details of the abductions are different, the pain of the families left behind is one and the same. My husband and I traded stories of our experiences with the other families, whom we met for the first time on the day we established the association.

Because Megumi was a child when she disappeared, the search for her was intensive and conducted on a large scale. However, for the families of the three couples, the circumstances were very different. Since the young people were all past the age of twenty, rumors had circulated that the couple had eloped because their parents disapproved of their relationship, or that they had disappeared because of money troubles. Even the police didn't dismiss these possibilities, so the families underwent a great deal of heartache from cruel rumors and speculation.

Kaoru Hasuike and Yukiko Okudo disappeared on July 31, 1978. Mr. Hasuike was a third-year student at Chuo University at the time, and he had returned to Kashiwazaki to spend part of his summer holiday at home.

When he left his house, he was riding his bicycle, wearing a T-shirt and a pair of shorts, and he told his grandmother that he would be eating dinner at home. That was the last anyone saw of him. Ms. Okudo was a beauty consultant at a cosmetics company. She had told her family that she would be meeting Kaoru Hasuike at six o'clock at the library. They would have tea together and then she would be home by eight o'clock, but she never returned. Kaoru's bicycle was later discovered in the bicycle rack in front of the library.

Kaoru had plans with his mother to watch his younger sister play in a tennis tournament the next day. And he didn't take his wallet or driver's license with him when he left home.

Since his home was near the ocean, his father feared that Kaoru might have drowned, and searched for him along the shore. When they heard that he was seen in a pachinko parlor in Nagoya, his father inquired at every pachinko parlor, taking his son's photo with him. The father once stood all day long in Tokyo's Sanya district, where the day laborers gathered, wondering if he might not see his son. For a long time after Kaoru's disappearance, his parents continued to pay his college tuition and the rent on his apartment. Kaoru's older brother has become the secretary of our association.

Mr. Chimura and Ms. Hamamoto of Obama City in Fukui Prefecture vanished together on July 7, 1978. The two were to be married in November, and had already reserved their reception hall. Both families were looking forward to their marriage, so there was no reason for them to elope.

Ms. Hamamoto had lost her parents when she was still young, and her older brother had acted as her guardian. It was her brother who became a member of the Families Association. Because a character in Ms. Hamamoto's first name also appears in the Korean name of the Japanese woman who taught Kim Hyon Hui (the woman responsible for bombing the Korean Airlines flight) it was once speculated that the Japanese instructor was Ms. Hamamoto. Her brother received numerous requests for interviews until investigations proved otherwise.

As for Mr. Chimura's family, his mother became ill with grief after her son's disappearance and has since become bed-ridden. Because Mr. Chimura's siblings live far away, his father looks after her all by himself.

I once asked to meet Mr. Chimura's mother, and we met at her home when the Association for the Rescue of Abductees gathered in the town of Obama. Mr. Chimura's father must have spoken often about us, for when he said, "Mrs. Yokota is here," Mrs. Chimura held out her hand and cried that she had wanted to see us. I cried too as I held her hand tightly. She needed to be helped to a sitting position, but I told her, "I have not given up hope, and I will do all I can. Please don't give up hope, either, and try to get well."

My husband and I are blessed with good health, so we can go on. It is the hardest for those families who are experiencing illness. My heart goes out to these parents when I think of their worries.

I once shared a room with Kaoru Hasuike's mother after the Association for Rescue met in Niigata on April 18, 1999. Late into the night, Mrs. Hasuike confided to me the heartache she has borne since her son vanished. No words can really convey this pain, but I have experienced it too. Her words went straight to my heart.

Shuichi Ichikawa's parents have related that, after their son disappeared, they put away all of his clothes in boxes. They never opened these boxes again until newspaper reporters came to their home. How agonizing it must have been to open a box, to see the clothes, and to detect the lingering scent of their son after a span of twenty years.

Until we formed the association, each family was alone with its pain. Not knowing whether our sons, daughters, or sisters were alive or dead was bad enough, but we have also had to endure heartless rumors concerning our loved ones. When we met for the first time, we promised one another that we would help each other keep our spirits up, and somehow bring back our loved ones so that our families could be reunited.

Since the establishment of the association, I have set out with the others to lobby government offices and agencies, to collect signatures for petitions, and to appeal for help at the various gatherings set up by branches of the Association for Rescue all over the country. Until then, we had been alone in our sorrow. I cannot tell you how much strength it has given me to be able to meet others who have shared the same pain, and to be able to turn to each other for support.

A Million Signatures

It was Mr. Kojima's idea to collect signatures to petition the government for a speedy resolution to the plight of the abducted. On March 13, 1997, an appeal submitted by Mr. Kojima, entitled "Support the Rescue Megumi Movement," appeared in the announcements column of the *Sankei Shimbun* newspaper. Many readers responded that they would like to help, and asked us to send them signature forms.

We decided to take an active part in the signature collection campaign as well, and asked the Governor of Niigata, Ikuo Hirayama, to be the first to sign. Mr. Kojima added an appeal for donations to support the movement. But as Megumi's parents, we thought it appropriate to bear the cost of our activities ourselves, so we did not include the appeal for donations in our petition forms, only a letter that explained our objectives.

We began to send out our appeal at the end of March. We sent them to our relatives, my husband's acquaintances from his banking days, my school alumnae, my colleagues at the company where I had worked a long time ago, colleagues of our sons, Megumi's classmates from elementary school and middle school, as well as my friends at church.

We soon received a flood of responses. Every day, my doorbell rang and I received bundles of letters. We lived in an apartment, and because all the mail couldn't fit into our mailbox, our mail carrier delivered them right to our door. As she handed me the letters, she would say to me, "Good luck, Mrs. Yokota."

Some people gathered so many signatures that they put the forms in a box and sent them to us by parcel delivery.

Every evening, my husband and I would go over the forms. We would number each page, and if a signature were missing from a line, we would make a note of it. My husband is very precise, and he numbered each page meticulously. But by the time the clock read 1:00 a.m., I would be sleepy and occasionally miss numbers. Finally, we would gather the pages into bundles of one hundred pages each, tie them up and label the number of signatures in the bundle.

My husband and I repeated this operation for many nights. We would often receive letters of encouragement with the signed forms, and it was my job to write letters expressing our appreciation.

We had decided that the deadline for the first round of the signature campaign would be the end of May, two months after the start. Within those two months, we gathered 255,000 signatures. We were full of gratitude for all the people who signed our petition. When we sent the forms to Mr. Kojima on June 5, we filled eleven cartons. The delivery person came with a trolley cart to pick up the cartons, and commented on how heavy they were. I think each box weighed about 18 kilograms. Mr. Kojima also received about 250,000 signatures.

On May 5, my husband and I, along with the parents of Kaoru Hasuike, stood on a popular shopping street called Bandai City in Niigata to ask pedestrians to sign our petition. It was the first time we had ever done such a thing.

When we arrived, Mr. Kojima and the volunteers at the Association for Rescue had already put up large poster boards with blown-up photos of Megumi and Kaoru. They had also prepared sashes emblazoned with our names to drape across our chests, similar to those that political candidates wear during election campaigns. One was for me. It read, "Mother, Sakie Yokota," and the other, for my husband, read, "Father, Shigeru Yokota." They had also set up a loudspeaker.

I was slightly taken aback when I saw all of this, but after I was instructed to put the sash on, and the microphone was thrust into my hand, I felt impelled to do my best. One of the members of the Association for Rescue spoke out and introduced us: "The parents of Megumi Yokota are here. I hope that you will all give them your support." These words spurred me on, and I joined my husband to ask passersby to sign our petition.

Since many people from the media were also covering the event, the pedestrians stood off at a distance at first. Someone noticed this and asked the press to move a little farther away. Soon, many people lined up at the tables and painstakingly signed their names to our petition. I think people in Niigata remembered the abductions of Megumi and Kaoru Hasuike because the incidents took place in their locality.

On May 25, another signature campaign kicked off in Kashiwazaki, the hometown of the Hasuike family. On June 7, a large Association for Rescue meeting was held in the Bandai civic center of Niigata City to appeal for help in the repatriation of the victims. The parents of Kaoru Hasuike and Yukiko Okudo, as well as the mother of Takeshi Terakoshi of Ishikawa attended, and again, we gathered a great many signatures.

Within a short time, half a year from the start of our movement, we had gathered a total of 570,000 signatures. In August, we delivered the signed petition forms to the Prime Minister's residence. We gathered more signatures, over one million in total, and on April 17, 1998, we submitted the signed forms to the Foreign Minister at the time, Keizo Obuchi.

Here, I would like to explain a little about Takeshi Terakoshi, whose mother I became acquainted with at the meeting in Niigata City.

Takeshi is another Japanese who has been unable to return from North Korea. He went fishing with his two uncles in 1963 but never returned. Takeshi was thirteen years old and in his second year of middle school when he disappeared. The morning after they disappeared, their boat was discovered, but it was damaged as if it had hit something.

In 1987, some twenty-four years after their disappearance, his mother received a letter from Takeshi and his uncle telling her that they were in North Korea. Takeshi's mother had given him up for dead and had already had a funeral for him.

That year, accompanied by a Diet member, Takeshi's mother went to North Korea to see her son. By then, Takeshi was married with children. He told his mother that their ship had met with an accident, and when he regained consciousness, he was in a hospital in North Korea. His mother thought that Takeshi and his uncles had been rescued by a North Korean ship, but circumstances now suggest that they were abducted because their ship had accidentally come across a North Korean vessel on an espionage mission.

Mrs. Terakoshi has been to North Korea seven times to see her son. Each time, he reassures her that he is well. From time to time, however, she says that her son asks her to send him money. It has to be difficult for her to help him financially on her meager pension.

Whether he was rescued or abducted, I am sure that the meetings with her son were bittersweet since she could see him only under the surveillance of guards.

Warm Encouragement and Support

In 1997, branches of Association for Rescue were established in various cities throughout Japan, so that the movement was no longer confined to Niigata. My husband and I attended all the rallies to ask for support in our rescue attempt. Before and after the rallies, we also asked people to sign our petition. We have attended such rallies in Ashiya, Tokyo, Osaka, Kumamoto, Fukuoka, Miyazaki, Obama in Fukui, Kashiwazaki City in Niigata, Kobe, Kagoshima, Kyoto, Chuo University, Sapporo, Fukui, Nagasaki and Yashiro in Kumamoto. Signature rallies have also been held in various cities, and my husband and I have attended these events, too.

We are especially indebted to Sachinori Sato for his help in our signature rally. Mr. Sato is a teacher at a middle school in Hachioji city of Tokyo. His younger sister was a friend of Megumi's, and his father worked for the Bank of Japan, as did my husband. We spent time in each other's company when both our families were posted in Niigata. When we were newly transferred to Niigata, Mr. Sato's sister came to our house to take Megumi to her new school. Shortly after we moved to Niigata, Mr. Sato's family was transferred to Nagoya. I remember that, after their move, Megumi and I had talked about how much we missed them.

Mr. Sato coached the table tennis club at his school, and the students from his club once held a signature rally at a station in Tokyo. That day, it rained so hard that the forms became soaked. In spite of the terrible weather, the students stood with their umbrellas over their heads and called out loudly to pedestrians, asking them to sign the petition. Just seeing them standing there, making their appeals so earnestly and wearing a school uniform that was the same navy color as Megumi's, made me feel like crying. I was full of gratitude for what they were doing.

When we finished, I invited them to have a bite to eat because I knew that they were hungry and cold. The students later wrote to thank me for the pasta we ate together. They told me that it tasted delicious, and that they would like to do it all again.

Later, when I heard that they were going to play in a table tennis tournament, I sent them soft drinks. They wrote me again and said that, before drinking the soda, they had pledged that they were going out there to win the competition. They were very excited and happy when they actually won.

Mr. Sato told me that some of the students wanted to visit us and asked if they could do so. When I replied that I would be glad to have them, about ten students came to our home. They sang songs and played the piano that my son had played, and we spent a pleasant afternoon in their company. All the students were truly kind and fun to be with.

Another person to whom we are indebted is Mr. Yoshie Baba, the former principal of Megumi's elementary school, Niigata Elementary. He read the newspaper account of our first signature campaign, held on May 5. It was a campaign in which a lot of

Megumi's friends had volunteered, standing on the street with us to ask for signatures. He also happened to live near Mr. Kojima, so he had immediately contacted us to offer his help.

I remember that on the first day Megumi went to her new school, she came home and, with characteristic spiritedness, said, "Mother, the principal at the new school is really neat!" I asked her what she meant by that, and she told me that he looked like a film star. Mr. Baba hasn't changed at all since those days, and I recall Megumi's words whenever I see him.

Megumi had transferred to Niigata Elementary in the second term of her sixth year, so she attended the school for only a short while. Mr. Baba, for his part, was going to be transferred to another school after Megumi's grade had graduated. Though they didn't know each other for very long, he has written for *The Sound of the Sea*, the Association newsletter published by Mr. Kojima.

Mr. Baba wrote that he still remembers handing Megumi her elementary school diploma. In August 1999, he also wrote a four-page letter in English to President Clinton in which he asked the president to help rescue his former student from her tragic predicament. It was a moving letter relating how he had come to know Megumi and about the appeals and petitions for her return. "I cannot sit still knowing the stark reality of my former student's plight," he wrote. "The victims are not only Megumi, but countless other people from countries throughout the world. Please help us in our attempt to negotiate their return."

The newspaper *Niigata Nippo* wrote about his letter in its August 25, 1999 edition, along with Mr. Baba's comment: "I wanted to do anything that would take us a step closer to the release of the victims. That's when I thought of writing directly to the president."

Mr. Baba is present at all the rallies held by the Association throughout Japan. I am full of gratitude for his thoughts toward Megumi, though he only knew her for a short while, and for his selfless devotion to the effort to save his former ward.

The mother of the child who had found it difficult to go to school in Hiroshima was also very kind to Megumi while we lived there. In recent years, she has also been one of our staunch supporters. We had corresponded after we moved from Hiroshima, and when she learned of Megumi's disappearance, she vowed to give up her favorite beverage, coffee, until Megumi was found.

Shortly after Megumi's disappearance, she wrote me a six-page letter in which she described a mysterious dream she had had.

She dreamt that she had taken a trip to continental Asia with her friends and had become lost in a jungle. They became frightened when a band of soldiers appeared with rifles in their hands. But behind the soldiers, she saw a woman with long hair tied back in a ponytail, holding a baby. When she looked closely, it was Megumi. My friend was about to call out to her when Megumi signaled her to be quiet. She seemed to be telling my friend that she was all right, but that they should go back quickly the way they had come. My friend ran back with her friends and woke up.

I sometimes reread my friend's letter, and find myself hoping that wherever Megumi is, she is well. After we learned that Megumi was in North Korea, I shuddered to think that this might be what my friend's dream signified.

Recently, the friend sent me another letter in which she wrote that she had dreamt that the North Korean regime was changing. She encouraged me to keep up my spirits. I only wish that her dream would come true.

When I think about it, Megumi lived in Japan for only thirteen years, and it has been twenty years since she disappeared. We moved frequently, so it would not have been surprising if we lost touch with many of the people we became acquainted with in each place we lived. Yet, many of the people who are supporting us are the people who knew Megumi during those thirteen years. I find myself deeply grateful for their friendship and the mysterious ties that bind people together.

On April 14, 1999, during a visit to Kumamoto, we had the opportunity to speak to the students at Buntoku High School, a private school affiliated with the Kumamoto Institute of Technology.

The principal of the high school, Koji Abe, was a member of the Kumamoto Committee of the Association for Rescue, and his students had collected 30,000 signatures for our petition the previous summer.

When Katsumi Sato (Chairperson of the National Association for Rescue), my husband, and I entered the school's auditorium with the principal, we were surprised to see the number of students who had gathered there. I later heard that there were 1,300 students in all. These students sat for an hour and a half, listening to our story without making a sound.

I spoke of how Megumi had disappeared, and all that we did to try to find her. I described what it had been like for us the past twenty years, how it felt as parents to have a child disappear. I told them that their own parents would do exactly as we had done if anything happened to them, for that is how parents feel about their children. I ended by asking them to please listen to what their parents and teachers have to say, and to take good care of themselves.

Some of the girls began to cry as I talked. When our talk ended, the students stood up as one at a signal from a teacher and saw us off. As we walked toward the doorway, they clapped and some of them called out to us, "Good luck to you!" I was so moved that I left the auditorium crying.

We often hear how young people these days won't stop talking, even after class begins, but I realized then that the young are not all like that. Buntoku High School had a reputation as a wild and troubled school before Mr. Abe became its principal. Windows were broken and school spirit was at a low. I think that I saw for myself how young people can change, and that it all depends on having a good teacher or leader to show them the way.

Reunion with An Myon Jin

Since 1997, my husband and I have had the good fortune to meet many people whom we would never have met if it were not for Megumi. Again, if it were not for Megumi—if our lives had continued their normal course—we would never have met a former spy from North Korea by the name of An Myon Jin. Twenty years ago, spies in my mind only inhabited the realm of movies and novels. I could never have imagined that I would one day meet a real spy, and actually speak with one, face to face.

I have already mentioned our first meeting with Mr. An in Seoul, right after we learned that Megumi was in North Korea. I also wrote of the decision Mr. An had made to identify himself in the media, and to write a book in order to corroborate his statements. Mr. An defected to South Korea in August 1993.

People like Mr. An are trained to become spies at the Kim Jong Il Political and Military University. Specifically, they are taught how to conduct espionage in South Korea, which means becoming familiar with South Korean cities and lifestyles so that they will not be conspicuous and give themselves away. People in North Korea are taught that South Korea is a poverty-stricken country, and that they are very fortunate to live in the North. However, in the course of his training, Mr. An realized that things were not as he had been taught, and secretly planned his defection.

His opportunity came when he and three other

spies infiltrated South Korea on a reconnaissance mission. Once he had crossed the 38th parallel, he asked for asylum. It was a very risky undertaking, for if his accomplices suspected anything, they could have shot him; the South Korean border guards may have attempted to shoot him too, if they saw him trying to enter.

A defector rarely identifies himself by name because the North Korean authorities may exact revenge on the family left behind. There is also the possibility that the authorities will have the defector assassinated. Mr. An decided to reveal his identity and appear before the media, fully aware of the risk that he was taking.

In his book, *North Korean Abduction Operative* published in March 1998, he writes that he decided to reveal his identity after meeting us, because he was deeply moved by the ties that bind a parent and child. I am sure that he was motivated by his love for his homeland as well, but if it were not for his courageous and selfless decision, the truth about the whereabouts of Megumi and all the other victims would never have become known.

In July 1998, the National Association for the Rescue of Japanese Kidnapped by North Korea invited Mr. An to Japan. It had been suggested in the spring of that year to invite Mr. An to testify at a session of the Diet, but unfortunately, that did not happen.

On July 31, my husband and I went to Niigata Airport to welcome Mr. An to Japan. We also took part in a press conference at the airport's VIP lounge.

While Mr. An had seemed nervous when we first met in Seoul a year and a half ago, the man who met us this time returned our greeting with a warm smile. Our first impression of his sincere personality did not change, however. At the press conference he answered each question carefully, and if he didn't know something, he was not afraid to say so. Here is part of his statement at the press conference:

> To be frank, until three years ago I thought that the North Korean abduction of Japanese people was a legitimate undertaking, that it was necessary in order to realize the reunification of the North and South. So I feel I owe an apology because I didn't treat these people with any sympathy when I saw them in the North. In North Korea, I had been taught that the division of the two Koreas was largely the result of Japanese actions, so I thought that it was right that the Japanese people should pay the price for reunification.
>
> (From the Association Newsletter, No. 5)

When I read Mr. An's statement, I became deeply fearful of the totalitarian authority that could teach a bright and honest young man like Mr. An to submit to a dogma, to follow blindly regardless of the consequences. If these young people had received more genuine, humanistic educations, they could have fulfilled the roles they were truly destined for. This is a tragedy that has made me reflect on the correlations between politics and education.

Until his return to Seoul on August 10, Mr. An presented his testimony in Niigata, Kashiwazaki, Tokyo, Kobe, Kagoshima, and Fukuoka. He visited the places where Megumi, Kaoru Hasuike, Yukiko Okudo, Shuichi Ichikawa and Rumiko Masumoto had been abducted, and attended several press conferences.

My husband and I accompanied him throughout his visit, and in Fukuoka, our older son joined us for lunch. My son thought that he and Mr. An might be able to speak directly to each other without the aid of a translator if he could speak English, and asked me what I thought. I told my son that Mr. An was an intelligent man so it might be possible, but we found out that Mr. An was not conversant in English. Despite that, the two of them had a very earnest conversation through the interpreter.

My son had heard that in Germany, when two people make a vow to work together, it is a custom to exchange something of sentimental value. When my son asked if there is a similar practice in Korea, Mr. An quickly removed his watch and handed it to my son, saying, "Let us place our watches in each other's keeping until Megumi's return."

Mr. An must have thought that my son meant exchanging something valuable. Unfortunately, my son did not have his watch on him that day. So, at the end of our lunch, my husband and I went to my son's house for his watch and gave it to Mr. An at his hotel.

Mr. An and my twin sons were born in the same month of the same year, just three days apart. Mr. An had risked his life for what he believed. It was unlikely my sons could aspire to do the same. However, I think that it is one of life's mysterious coincidences that a man almost exactly the same age as my sons would testify on behalf of my daughter. We are happy to hear that Mr. An is now happily married in South Korea, and has settled into his new life. During the press conference at the Niigata Airport, Mr. An also made the following statement:

> I believe that there are other people in South Korea who can give factual testimony concerning North Korea's abduction of foreigners. However, these people do not want to talk about these occurrences because they do not want to get involved.
>
> When I see these people, my heart aches with shame, and I also feel some contempt. I am deeply disappointed at their attitude, for if these people who know the truth only had the courage to speak, it would be a great help to these families in Japan who have had their loved ones taken. If the Japanese government demanded a resolution with greater insistence, and if these families and their friends in the Association raised their voices higher, perhaps these silent people would become convinced of the possibility for change, and be motivated to add their testimony.
>
> (From the Association Newsletter, No. 5)

I sometimes indulge in the dream that, if I had wings, I would be able to fly across the sea and rescue Megumi. I am prepared to do anything, no matter what the consequences may be to me, if only I could have Megumi back.

In reality, it may be as Mr. An has suggested. As long as there is insufficient motivation or will on the part of the defectors to speak up and present their testimony, the way may never open up for Megumi and the others to return.

However, I am determined to do all that I can possibly do, to never lose hope, and to believe that the day will surely come when I am reunited with my daughter. I will wait for that day.

EPILOGUE

A Legacy of Dignity

The news is full of outrageous and incomprehensible events. A while ago, the younger sister of someone killed in the sarin gas attack in Matsumoto was kidnapped and threatened with death. In the Kyrgyz Republic, formerly part of the USSR, several Japanese engineers were kidnapped. The cowardice of these acts makes me so angry that I can almost feel myself trembling. My heart goes out to the victims' families for the pain they are suffering.

When a beloved child, husband, wife, father or mother is kidnapped out of the blue, those left behind blame themselves for everything they did or didn't do, and yearn to know what has happened to their loved ones. The family members left behind become frustrated when their efforts lead nowhere, and ultimately, when there is little more they can do, the feeling of powerlessness fills their hearts with pain.

More than two years have passed since I learned, in January 1997, that my missing daughter is alive in North Korea. Suddenly, we were confronted with the political realities of international relations. In these two years, however, many people have come forward to support the families of the abducted victims. And thanks to their enlightened efforts, many more people have become aware of this issue and the country responsible for the abductions, North Korea.

My husband and I have taken part in the effort to focus public attention on the abductions and their consequences. On May 2, 1999, we attended a large rally—the National Rally to Make the Rescue of Japanese Kidnapped by North Korea the First Priority of National Policy—held at the Hibiya Kokaido Public Hall, a major venue in Tokyo. My husband and Katsumi Sato, Chairperson of the National Association for the Rescue of Japanese Kidnapped by North Korea, led the executive committee to plan this rally, and 130 journalists, business leaders, and other influential people from all walks of life lent their support. Well-known journalist Yoshiko Sakurai became the representative of the supporters.

The rally was also attended by the families of Kaoru Hasuike, Yukiko Okudo, Yasushi Chimura, Shuichi Ichikawa, Rumiko Masumoto and Keiko Arimoto, as well as the families of two South Korean victims of abduction. Lee Young-wook's son was abducted while he was studying abroad. Kim Te-ju lost her husband, a commercial fisherman. Their daughter, Chu Wu-yon, accompanied her mother.

Mr. Lee is a lawyer who is about the same age as my husband. He conversed with us in fluent Japanese. His son had been studying business at the Massachusetts Institute of Technology, but during the summer, Mr. Lee had sent his son to Europe so that he could absorb a little of European culture. His son was abducted while visiting Austria.

Mrs. Kim's husband was caught when he crossed the 38th parallel in pursuit of fish. Under normal circumstances, a South Korean fisherman can be released upon paying a fine if North Korean authorities are satisfied that he is not a spy. It so happened, however, that the Kim Myong Chol family had chosen to defect from North Korea at around the same time, and the North Korean government made the outrageous demand of exchanging Mrs. Kim's husband for the Kim Myong Chol family. The South Korean government refused, so Mrs. Kim's husband was thrown into a concentration camp on trumped up charges that he was a spy.

After the assembly, I accompanied Mrs. Kim and her daughter on a shopping excursion in Shinjuku. Twenty-nine-year-old Chu was fluent in Japanese, and had a very friendly personality. She was five years younger than Megumi, but I thought to myself as I walked with them that when Megumi comes back, she would be like Chu, able to speak both Korean and Japanese. It was a pleasant outing.

The assembly was held in the middle of a long weekend, so I worried whether many people would attend. Until the day before the event, my husband and I worked into the night, sending out announcements and calling friends.

I hoped that we would be able to fill at least the main floor, but I couldn't be sure because when we reached the hall at 10:30, we were led directly to a waiting room. Just before the assembly was to begin, someone from the planning committee told us that the hall was full, with people filling the second and third tiers as well. When we looked out from the wings, we could see that the hall was indeed full of people, and I felt tremendous gratitude. I later learned that almost two thousand people had attended.

The assembly opened with Mikiko Minami acting as MC. She is a writer and one of our supporters. A choir of volunteers sang a song, "Let This Voice Reach Our Children, Our Friends" that had been composed by Kuni Saito, Megumi's chorus teacher at her elementary school in Niigata. Another song, written by three young people living in Osaka, was sung at the close of the gathering, "A Prayer to Return Home," accompanied by their guitars. I was moved that young people such as these singers were also taking part in our effort to bring home our loved ones.

After Kuni Saito's chorus, my husband and then the Korean families addressed the assembly. This was followed by a discussion moderated by the journalist, Yoshiko Sakurai. Katsumi Sato, the columnist Taro

Yayama, military expert Mamoru Sato, and Yoshie Baba, the former principal of Niigata Elementary School, presented their views on the abduction issue.

Next, the families made their appeal. All the families were seated in the second tier, so we carefully but quickly made our way down the stairs to the stage. I had never spoken in front of such a large number of people. Fortunately, the hall was dark and I was not able to see the crowd; otherwise, I could never have stopped my trembling legs. Mustering my strength, I spoke:

> Twenty-two years ago, my daughter, Megumi, was locked up in the hold of a ship and abducted to North Korea. I have heard that throughout the voyage, she screamed, "Mother, Mother" and clawed the walls until her nails came off. What an absolutely terrifying experience it must have been for her. Since then, my husband and I cannot shake the feeling that Megumi is calling to us, asking us why we haven't come for her. We have spent many painful, dreadful days. I ask for your help in realizing our dream to be reunited with our daughter as quickly as possible.

As I focused all my energy on speaking, I forgot where I was and, in the darkness, I could see Megumi crying "Mother!" I felt the tears rolling down my face.

The other families followed. They were the parents and brother of Kaoru Hasuike, the father of

Yukiko Okudo, the father of Yasushi Chimura, Shuichi Ichikawa's brother and his wife, the father and siblings of Rumiko Masumoto, and the parents of Keiko Arimoto.

The aging parents pleaded in voices choked with emotion for help in rescuing their children, while the siblings criticized the Japanese government, quietly yet passionately, asking why the government hadn't taken a stronger stance on this issue with the North Korean government. Their anger and frustration are feelings we all share.

Megumi is not simply a child gone missing. With effort, there is a chance of finding a family member who has run away from home, been kidnapped, or gone into hiding. But Megumi and the others were pulled away from their families by such a powerful entity that we are helpless as individuals.

In 1978, the year after Megumi disappeared, three young couples mysteriously disappeared, and a fourth couple had the harrowing experience of almost being kidnapped. I can't imagine why no one became more suspicious, when all the incidents were so similar, and all took place within months, even weeks, of each other.

What makes their disappearances truly a tragedy is that the government has chosen to do nothing to help the victims; it has turned a blind eye for twenty years to these horrendous crimes. I am full of sorrow that while the young people who were abducted must have longed for their homeland, their country first ignored the suspicious circumstances, then the fact of their abduction, for these many years.

When I was growing up, a father wielded stern power as the head of the family. He exercised his authority to teach us to despise deceit and cowardice, and to value justice. No matter how young we were, if we showed lapses in defending these moral values or willfully advanced our own desires at the expense of what was just or true, my father would not hesitate to discipline us, boys and girls alike.

We were also taught in the course of our everyday lives to treasure life in all forms, no matter how small, whether it was plant or animal, and to appreciate the beauty of nature. Both my father and my mother taught me reverence—to fear as well as to cherish the unseen power that sustains us all.

After the war, Japan struggled to recover from the unprecedented destruction war had wreaked. Now, Japan is rich in material wealth, and the Japanese are privileged to lead peaceful lives free of want. Yet I cannot help but feel that during the transition from poverty to wealth, something of great value was lost or forgotten.

In our present situation, there is only one thing we can do, and that is to continue our appeal to the government to rescue our families. But the government is made up of individuals, and there is something that I would like to say to those who are responsible for negotiations with North Korea.

Many of you are people of my generation, brought up by stern fathers who took pride in our country and culture, and who instilled in you the same values my father taught me. I ask you to remember this legacy, the valuable lessons of dignity and integrity. I ask you to find those values again in your hearts, and act with courage to help us rescue those who were so cruelly taken away from us. Bring them back as soon as possible, for these people are, after all, your countrymen and women.

Representing all our supporters, Yoshiko Sakurai wrote the following in the rally announcement as her appeal for support:

> Twenty-two years have passed since the inexplicable disappearance of thirteen-year-old Megumi Yokota.
>
> In the early 1980s the media began reporting on the series of strange disappearances of young couples from the beaches along the Sea of Japan and in Kagoshima.
>
> In 1988, Seiroku Kajiyama, then Chairman of the National Public Safety Commission, said during a session of the Diet that these mysterious disappearances "strongly suggest abductions by North Korea."
>
> And then, in February 1997, when no one knew whether Megumi was still alive or long dead, it was revealed at a session of the Diet that a woman resembling Megumi had been seen in North Korea. Later, the government acknowledged

that the number of Japanese abducted to North Korea, including Megumi, were a total of 10 people in 7 separate incidents.

If the government was clearly aware of these facts, it had the obligation to rescue these victims, and to give their rescue top priority. The reason, quite obviously, is that the first responsibility of the government is to protect the lives of its citizens, their human rights, and their property.

What has the government done, then? The reality is this: The Japanese government has failed to be decisive in its negotiations with North Korea, and has continued aid to that country within the framework of its diplomatic relationships with the United States and South Korea.

Japan has sent rice to North Korea as humanitarian aid. Separately, Japan agreed to send another shipment of rice in a tacit exchange for the return of a handful of "wives from Japan." Furthermore, Japan has promised financial aid of one billion dollars, earmarked for the construction of a light-water nuclear reactor in North Korea.

Putting aside the question of how North Korea intends to use this nuclear reactor, the Japanese government's actions were overtures for peace and intended as humanitarian aid to the people of North Korea. I have no intention of opposing aid to ease the suffering of the people of North Korea. Rather, taking into account the multitudes of people facing severe and inescapable hardship, one is moved to sympathize.

However, it must never be forgotten under any circumstance that the welfare of one's own citizens comes first. The government's most important responsibility is to protect the lives of its people, to guarantee their safety, safeguard their human rights and defend them from any crimes that would compromise those rights.

The Japanese government has an obligation to protect its own citizens before it even considers undertaking activities for the greater good in the international community.

It has been two years since the Diet was informed of Megumi's presence in North Korea. Eleven years have passed since the government suspected, and then declared, that the missing people had been targets of "an abduction plotted by the North Korean government."

After twenty-two years in captivity, thirteen-year-old Megumi has become 35 years old.

The missing couple, Yasushi Chimura and Fukie Hamamoto, were twenty-three years old and soon to be married when they were kidnapped. They are now 44 years old.

The university student Kaoru Hasuike and his girlfriend Yukiko Okudo, as well as Shuichi Ichikawa and Rumiko Masumoto, were also in their twenties and just embarking on their adult lives with the bright energy of youth. They must now be in their mid-forties.

So many years have passed, and yet there has been no progress in the attempt to rescue these people, or others who are missing and thought to have been abducted. How can we rescue them?

It is a fact that Japan has no formal diplomatic relations with North Korea. It is also a fact that this makes it extremely difficult to negotiate with North Korea.

These are the very reasons why it is so important that members of the government overcome their ideological and political differences and ensure that the return of the abducted victims is given top priority in crafting national policy. The complex nature of the situation demands that the government put all its efforts into solving it. The prospect of a daunting negotiation, in which the outcome is hard to predict, requires strong political will and unflinching personal courage. When the situation looks hopeless, remember the victims in North Korea, robbed of their freedom, unable to return home, forbidden to communicate their existence to their families, and bearing their solitude alone.

If the government does nothing to save Megumi and the others, the very basis for its existence and even the concept of nationhood will be called into question. Only by demanding the return of all those who were abducted can our government claim its right to govern, and only with their safe return can our country claim to be a sovereign nation in fact. Let us overcome the individual differences that separate us, speak as one voice, and rescue our countrymen and women.

Ms. Sakurai's appeal is the voice deep in the hearts of all families robbed of their loved ones. We, the families, hope sincerely that those responsible for the negotiations are prepared to resolve this issue once and for all, united by a sense of justice, purpose, and courage.

This book is the translation of a work that the author published in Japanese in 1999.

For many years, and even after the book's publication in Japan, many Japanese dismissed rumors regarding abduction operations as a manifestation of Cold War paranoia. They were proven wrong when in 2002, under international pressure, North Korea's Chairman Kim publicly admitted to having whisked away foreign citizens.

North Korea has refused to return Megumi Yokota, claiming that she is dead, but the "evidence" they have provided has not substantiated their assertion. Author Sakie continues to have faith.

In 2006, Patty Kim and Chris Sheridan's documentary *Abduction: The Megumi Yokota Story*, based partly on an early translation manuscript of this memoir, won multiple awards at film festivals across America.

The abduction issue as a whole has hardly been resolved and continues to evolve, with new developments and greater awareness accruing each year.

The timeline that follows provides further details and a partial update on the international scandal.

The Kidnappings and their Historical Background: a Timeline

The Koreas and Japan		The World
• End of World War II; administration of Korean peninsula by the Soviet Union in the north and United States in the south.	**1945**	
• Syngman Rhee becomes the first president of South Korea, officially the Republic of Korea; Kim Il-sung becomes president of North Korea, officially the Democratic People's Republic of Korea.	**1948**	• United Nations proclaims Universal Declaration of Human Rights.
	1949	• Chinese communist party establishes the People's Republic of China.
• Start of Korean War.	**1950**	
• Stalemate in Korean War and armistice.	**1953**	• Stalin dies, halting the terrors but leaving a totalitarian state.
• The Red Cross Societies of Japan and North Korea arrange for Koreans living in Japan to repatriate to North Korea.[1]	**1959**	
• Military coup in South Korea inaugurates two decades of authoritarian rule.	**1961**	
	1962	• Cuban missile crisis highlights Cold War tensions.
	1963	• John F. Kennedy assassinated.
	1965	• America escalates bombing in North Vietnam.
• North Korean agents hijack a Korean Air Lines domestic flight. Twelve of the fifty-one passengers and crew are detained in North Korea.	**1969**	

1970

- Members of the Japanese Red Army hijack Japan Airlines Flight 351, a domestic flight, to fly to North Korea and defect.[2]

- North Korea becomes an increasingly authoritarian state under Kim Il-sung, who proclaims a new socialist constitution that names him President.

1972

- Richard Nixon's historic visit to the People's Republic of China.

1975

- Fall of Saigon; end of the Vietnam War.

1977

- Jimmy Carter becomes U.S. President.

- Hiroshi Kume (52)[3] disappears[4] from the Ushitsu Beach area in Ishikawa Prefecture in September.[5]

- In October, Kyoko Matsumoto (29) of Tottori Prefecture disappears after leaving her home to attend a knitting class near by.[6]

- Megumi Yokota (13) disappears from the city of Niigata in November.[7]

---

1 In the absence of diplomatic ties between the two countries, the Red Cross arranged for Korean residents in Japan to relocate to North Korea. Economic hardship in Japan and descriptions of North Korea as a "workers' paradise" convinced many to go. Between 1959 and 1984, a total of 93,340 people, including some 1,800 Japanese women married to Koreans, relocated. An estimated 6,800 spouses and children of Japanese nationality are thought to be living in North Korea.

2 Nine members of the Red Army Faction of the Japanese Communist League hijacked a Japan Airlines Boeing 727 ("Yodo"), announced their intention to defect to North Korea, and demanded to be flown there. Of the 129 hostages on the flight, the hijackers released all 122 passengers and flight attendants at Fukuoka and Seoul, South Korea, but took Shinjiro Yamamoto, the Vice Minister of Transport who volunteered to take their place. Yamamoto and the flight crew later returned safely to Japan, but the hijackers were granted asylum by North Korea.

3 All ages are the ages of abductees at the time of their disappearance.

4 The Japanese government considers all Japanese citizens described here as having "disappeared" to be victims of abduction by North Korea. Although the Japanese government officially recognizes 17 citizens to be abductees, there are numerous other cases in which the possibility of abduction cannot be ruled out. One estimate places the number of abductees at 260, another as high as 450.

5 Although North Korea categorically denies that Kume ever entered its borders, Japanese investigators have had an international warrant issued for the arrest of Kim Se-ho, the North Korean agent believed to have played a major role in Kume's abduction, and are demanding his extradition. The North Korean government claims "no knowledge of such a person." In comprehensive bilateral talks in February 2006, however, officials responded that they would conduct investigations to find out who is, pending the receipt of relevant information from the Japanese government.

6 Matsumoto was officially added to the list of abductees in November 2006. Since that time, the Japanese government has demanded her return and full disclosure regarding her disappearance, but the North Korean government has not responded to date.

7 At the third working-level bilateral meetings held in November 2004, North Korean officials submitted to the Japanese delegation ashes which they claimed were the remains of Megumi Yokota, who they reported died in April 1994. Tests revealed, however, that the ashes contained at least some DNA from some other individual. In April 2006, separate DNA tests conducted by the Japanese government revealed with a high degree of certainty that the father of Yokota's daughter was Kim Yong-nam, a South Korean abducted by North Korea in 1978 when he was still a high school student.

...

1978

- Minoru Tanaka (28) disappears. He is believed to have left Japan for Europe in June. He is believed to have disappeared from Japan, also in June.[9]
- In July, Yasushi Chimura (23) and Fukie Hamamoto (23) disappear after leaving their homes, telling their families that they have a date.[10] Kaoru Hasuike (20) and Yukiko Okudo (22) also disappear, this time from Niigata Prefecture.[11]
- In August, Shuichi Ichikawa (23) and Rumiko Masumoto (24) disappear after going to a local beach in Kagoshima Prefecture to watch the sun set.[12] Miyoshi Soga (46) and her daughter Hitomi (19) disappear from Niigata Prefecture after a shopping excursion.[15] Another young couple is almost abducted from a beach in Toyama Prefecture.

1979

- U.S. resumes diplomatic relations with China; formal relations with Taiwan are severed. The Soviet Union invades Afghanistan.

1980

- The *Sankei Shimbun* runs a front page story in January suggesting that "foreign intelligence agents" may have been involved in the disappearance of couples from coastal areas along the Sea of Japan, implicating North Korea for the first time.
- Toru Ishioka (22) and Kaoru Matsumoto (26) are believed to have disappeared from Europe in May.[14]
- In June, Tadaaki Hara (43) is kidnapped from Miyazaki Prefecture by North Korean agent Shin Gwang-soo.[15]

1981

- Ronald Reagan becomes U.S. President.

1983

- Keiko Arimoto (23) is believed to have disappeared from Europe in July.[16]

1986

- Megumi Yokota and South Korean abductee Kim Yong-nam are married in August, according to information released by North Korea in 2004.

1987

● Yokota gives birth to a daughter, Kim Hye-gyong (later changed to Eun-gyong), in September, according to information released by North Korea in 2004.

8 Tanaka was officially added to the list of abductees in April 2005. Since that time, the Japanese government has demanded his return and full disclosure regarding his disappearance, but the North Korean government has not responded to date.

9 Kim Hyon Hui (also spelled Hyeonhee), a North Korean agent convicted in the November 1987 bombing of Korean Air Flight 858, has testified that she learned to speak and act like a Japanese from a woman she knew as Li Un-hae. Japanese authorities believe that this woman was Taguchi. North Korean officials have confirmed that Taguchi did live in North Korea, and disclosed that she married Tadaaki Hara (another Japanese abductee) in 1984. They also claim that she died in a vehicle accident soon after Hara's death from illness in 1986, but have offered no documentation or other evidence to support these claims.

10 The two were married in North Korea in 1979. They were allowed to return to Japan in October 2002, and were joined by their daughter and two sons in May 2004. Japanese authorities have had an international warrant issued for the arrest of Shin Gwang-soo, the North Korean agent who played a major role in their abduction, and are demanding his extradition.

11 The two were married in North Korea in 1980. They were also allowed to return to Japan in October 2002, and were joined by their daughter and son in May 2004. Japanese authorities have had international warrants issued in February 2006 for the arrest of Choe Seungcheol, the North Korean agent who played a major role in their abduction, and in February 2007 for two accomplices, and are demanding their extradition from North Korea.

12 Officials in North Korea claim that the two married in July 1979, but that Ichikawa died of a heart attack in September that year, and that Masumoto also died of a heart attack in 1981. No documentation or other evidence has been offered in support of these claims.

13 Hitomi Soga was among the five Japanese allowed to return to Japan in October 2002. Her American husband, Charles Jenkins, and their two daughters joined her in July 2004. North Korean authorities claim that Miyoshi Soga never entered North Korea, but Japanese authorities have had an international warrant issued in November 2006 for the arrest of the North Korean agent suspected of abducting her, a woman known as Kim Myonsuk, and the Japanese government is demanding her extradition.

14 In 1988, Ishioka's family received a letter postmarked in Poland, in which Ishioka says that he, Matsumoto, and Keiko Arimoto are living in North Korea. North Korean authorities claim that Ishioka and Arimoto both died in a gas explosion in November 1988, but no documents or other evidence has been submitted in support of this. North Korean officials also claim that Matsumoto died in a traffic accident in August 1996. On two occasions—in September 2002 and the third bilateral working-level meetings held in November 2004—the North Korean side submitted ashes which they say may be those of Matsumoto. However, tests revealed the DNA of some other person from at least part of this sample.

15 North Korean agent Shin Gwang-soo testified to South Korean authorities that he abducted Hara to North Korea. Japanese investigators had an international warrant issued for Shin's arrest on suspicion of traveling with false documents using Hara's name, and the Japanese government has demanded Shin's extradition from North Korea. Another arrest warrant was issued in April 2006 for his central role in the abductions, but North Korea is not only refusing to extradite him, but is praising him as a national hero. North Korean officials claim that Hara married Yaeko Taguchi in 1984, but died in 1986 of cirrhosis of the liver. No documentation or other evidence has been offered in support of these claims.

16 A Japanese woman named Megumi Yao testified in a Japanese court in 2002 that she persuaded Arimoto to go to North Korea on the pretext that she was being hired for a market research project. Yao had married one of the Japanese communists who hijacked Japan Air Lines Flight 351 (see footnote 2), and lived in North Korea with him for a time. Kimihiro Uomoto (formerly Abe), another of the hijackers, and a North Korean agent were implicated in Arimoto's abduction. Japanese investigators had an international warrant issued (September 2002) for Uomoto's arrest, and the Japanese government is demanding his extradition, but North Korea has yet to respond. North Korean officials claim that Arimoto died in November 1988 in the same gas explosion that claimed the life of Toru Ishioka, but no documents or other evidence has been submitted in support of this.

1987	• Bombing of a South Korean commercial plane, Korean Air Flight 858, by North Korean agents.[17]	
1988		• The Olympic Games begin in Seoul.
1989		• George H. W. Bush becomes U.S. President. • Chinese government cracks down on protesters in Tiananmen Square. • The Berlin Wall falls in November. • The Cold War is officially ended at U.S.-Soviet summit in Malta. North Korea loses the economic support of USSR as Soviet power declines.
1990	• South Korea and the Soviet Union resume diplomatic relations.	
1991	• Japan and North Korea begin talks in January with the aim of normalizing relations. In November, at the eighth round of talks, Japan requests an investigation regarding the identity of spy instructor Li Un-hae; the North Korean delegation breaks off talks in protest.	• Gulf War begins; coalition forces bomb Iraq. • Boris Yeltsin becomes President of Russia; dissolution of the Soviet Union.
1992	• North Korea withdraws from the Nuclear Non-Proliferation Treaty. • China and South Korea resume diplomatic relations.	• Signing of the Maastricht Treaty opens the way to the creation of the European Union.
1993	• North Korea test-fires the Nodong-1 missile; the missile lands in the Sea of Japan off the coast of the Noto Peninsula. • North Korea expels International Atomic Energy Agency (IAEA) investigators. Former President Carter meets with Kim Il-sung in Pyongyang and negotiates an agreement to stop North Korean processing of spent nuclear fuel.	• Bill Clinton becomes U.S. President.
1994	• Kim Il-sung dies; succeeded by son Kim Jong-il.	

1995

- Korean Peninsula Energy Development Organization (KEDO) founded to build nuclear power plants for North Korea; North Korea agrees to halt domestic nuclear programs in exchange.
- Massive flooding in North Korea contributes to famine through the remainder of the 90's.

1996

- North Korean submarine runs aground off coast of South Korea; its crew of armed guerillas battle South Korean troops.

1997

- *Sankei Shimbun* runs a front-page story on Megumi Yokota, disclosing that the girl who disappeared twenty years ago at age thirteen had been abducted to North Korea. The following month, the families of abductees form a liaison group to publicize the issue and press for government action.
- The Japanese government announces in May that North Korea is "strongly suspected" of having abducted ten Japanese citizens in seven separate incidents.
- Kim Jong-il becomes General Secretary of the ruling party of North Korea, strengthening hold on power and cult of personality.
- Hong Kong returns to Chinese rule.

1998

- North Korea fires a Taepodong-1 ballistic missile over Japan.

1999

- North Korean espionage vessel discovered in Japanese waters; Japanese Self Defense Forces fire warning shots.
- Vladimir Putin becomes President of Russia.

2000

- Japanese government announces that it will send rice to North Korea; the families of abductees and their supporters organize a sit-in in front of Foreign Ministry and Liberal Democratic Party offices in protest.

---

17 Korean Air Flight 858, scheduled to fly from Baghdad, Iraq, to Seoul, South Korea, via Abu Dhabi and Bangkok, exploded in midair, killing all on board. A North Korean agent named Kim Hyon Hui (also spelled Hyeonhee), who also went by the Japanese name Mayumi Hachiya, was arrested trying to leave Bahrain on a fake Japanese passport, and tried for the bombing. She testified that she had been coached to speak and act like a Japanese by a woman she knew as Li Un-hae. Based on their physical likeness, it is believed that Li Un-hae was Japanese abductee Yaeko Taguchi.

2001
- George W. Bush becomes U.S. President.
- Junichiro Koizumi becomes Prime Minister of Japan.
- Terrorists attack U.S. homeland on September 11.

- North Korean Red Cross announces that it is terminating its investigation of "missing persons."

2002
- President Bush denounces Iran, Iraq, and North Korea as an "axis of evil" in State of the Union address.

- A Japanese woman who lived in North Korea admits to having helped deceive Keiko Arimoto into going to North Korea.[18]
- Prime Minister Koizumi meets with Kim Jong-il in North Korea in first Japan-North Korea summit. Kim admits that "over-zealous elements" had abducted Japanese citizens to North Korea; officials claim that five are living in North Korea and eight others have died.
- The following month, North Korea allows the five surviving abductees[19] to "visit" Japan for the first time in twenty-four years. They are dissuaded from returning, although their children remain in North Korea.
- North Korea announces that it is reopening its nuclear-fuel reprocessing plant.

2003
- Operation Iraqi Freedom begins.

- North Korea announces withdrawal from Nuclear Non-Proliferation Treaty.
- United Nations Commission on Human Rights adopts a resolution calling for North Korea to end its human rights violations and resolve all issues relating to the abduction of foreigners.
- Kim Hye-gyong, daughter of abductee Megumi Yokota, is interviewed by a Japanese delegation in Pyongyang, North Korea.

2004
- Prime Minister Koizumi visits North Korea for a second Japan-North Korea summit. The children of four of the abductees who returned to Japan in 2002 are allowed to leave North Korea and join their parents in Japan.[20]

- Hitomi Soga, the fifth abductee who returned to Japan in 2002, is reunited with her husband and two daughters.[21]

2006

- Japanese delegation goes to North Korea for comprehensive bilateral talks.[22]
- Sakie Yokota, mother of Megumi, testifies in U.S. House of Representatives subcommittee regarding the abductions, and pleads for help in a meeting with President Bush.
- Shigeru Yokota, father of Megumi, and others travel to South Korea to meet with family of abductee Kim Yong-nam.
- North Korea fires seven missiles including the Taepodong-2.
- North Korea's state-run media, the Korean Central News Agengy, announces that an underground nuclear test has been conducted; China joins in international condemnation of North Korea's nuclear activities.

2007

- Vice President Dick Cheney meets with Shigeru and Sakie Yokota at the U.S. Embassy in Tokyo.

18 See footnote 16.

19 Kaoru Hasuike, Yukiko Hasuike (Okudo), Yasushi Chimura, Fukie Chimura (Hamamoto), and Hitomi Soga.

20 The Japanese government promises North Korea 250,000 tons of rice and US$10 million in humanitarian aid. Japan had provided humanitarian aid in the form of 50 tons of rice in 1995, 2000, and 2001, respectively.

21 Soga had married Charles Jenkins, an American soldier who had defected to North Korea during the Korean War. Japanese officials arranged for Soga to be reunited with her husband and two daughters in Indonesia, where they were persuaded to begin a new life in Japan.

22 Approximately eleven hours in total were spent discussing the issue of abductions. The Japanese delegation demanded once again the return of all surviving abductees, a commitment by North Korean authorities to reopen investigations into the abductions and the fate of all Japanese citizens, and the extradition of suspected kidnappers. North Korean officials repeated their claim that all survivors have returned to Japan, and refused to extradite any suspects.